At Hell's Gate

At Hell's Gate

*A Soldier's Journey
from War to Peace*

Claude Anshin Thomas

Shambhala
Boston & London 2004

Shambhala Publications, Inc.
Horticultural Hall
300 Massachusetts Avenue
Boston, Massachusetts 02115

© 2004 by Claude A. Thomas

Printed in the United States of America

Distributed in the United States by Random House, Inc., and in Canada
by Random House of Canada Ltd

ISBN 0-7394-5166-9

To my son, Zachary Alan Thomas,
whose presence and love has been the inspiration
for my healing and transformation

And to Susan Weisberg, for her tireless efforts in
assimilating materials from tapes, transcripts, and
writings so that this book could become what it is

Zen Master Guichen said, "Where are you going?"

Fayan replied, "On an ongoing pilgrimage."

Guichen said, "Why do you go on a pilgrimage?"

Fayan replied, "I don't know."

Guichen said, "Not knowing is most intimate."

—from The Record of Master Fayan Wenyi

Contents

Preface   xi

1   The Seeds of War   3

2   The Light at the Tip of the Candle   37

3   The Bell of Mindfulness   55

4   If You Blow Up a Bridge, Build a Bridge   70

5   Walking to Walk   99

6   Finding Peace   132

Appendix   155

Further Reading   163

Acknowledgments   165

The Zaltho Foundation   167

A Soldier's Prayer

At the age of seventeen I enlisted in the U.S. Army and volunteered for service in Vietnam. By taking up arms, I was directly responsible for killing several hundred people, and the killing didn't stop until I was honorably discharged and sent home with numerous medals, including a Purple Heart. But as I pieced together the shrapnel of my life and discovered the heart that had been shattered by combat, I discovered that there is no justified killing, no clear separation between good and bad violence, and no rectitude in war. War is just the acting out of suffering.

Arriving at this understanding and accepting the first Buddhist precept of not killing (which is also the fifth commandment), required a long march not only through Vietnam, homelessness, and jails but also through war-torn and war-scarred regions around the world, from Bosnia to Afghanistan, Auschwitz to Cambodia.

This book contains the field notes from those marches and my attempt to share the lessons I've learned, not only in the monasteries where I have trained, but in the trenches, streets, and homes where I discovered the truth of the Buddha's insight about the reality of suffering. We all desire happiness—what is good, pleasant, right, permanent, joyful, harmonious, satisfying, and easy. But life often brings frustration, dissatisfaction, incompleteness, and sorrow. It is this suffering that leads us to violence against ourselves and against others, and coming to terms with suffering is the only way ultimately to end violence and live with greater peace in the world.

I hope this book will be of benefit to those who are affected by violence and yearn for something different—peace. Everyone has their Vietnam. Everyone has their war. May we embark together on a pilgrimage of ending these wars and truly living peace.

At Hell's Gate

1

The Seeds of War

Imagine for a moment that you are standing outside in the rain. What do you typically think and feel as rain falls around you?

For me, every time it rains I walk through war. For two rainy seasons I experienced very heavy fighting. During the monsoons in Vietnam, the tremendous volume of water leaves everything wet and muddy. Now when it rains, I am still walking through fields of young men screaming and dying. I still see tree lines disintegrating from napalm. I still hear seventeen-year-old boys crying for their mothers, fathers, and girlfriends. Only after reexperiencing all of that can I come to the awareness that right now, it's just raining.

For lack of a better word, let's call these events flashbacks. They are a reliving of experiences that I have not yet come to terms with. I could be in a grocery store, reaching up to take a can of vegetables off the shelf, when I'm suddenly overwhelmed by fear because I think that the can might be booby-trapped. Rationally I know that this isn't true, but for one year, my tour of duty in Vietnam, I lived in an environment where this was a realistic fear—and to this day I am unable to process that wartime experience.

But this is not just my story. This happens every day all over the world. Every day there are people reliving war—reliving their own experiences of violence, calamity, childhood trauma.

Before we can get to a place of peace, we have to touch our suffering—embrace it and hold it. This is something I have been learning in recent years. But for many years before that, all I learned was how to make war.

A conditioning to violence

For my first seventeen years almost all my experiences watered the seeds of violence in me. War was everywhere. I was raised in a small town in Pennsylvania. My father, like most of the men in my town, had served in World War II. When that generation talked about war, they didn't speak truthfully. Unable to touch the deep and profound wounds that war had left inside them, they talked about war like a great adventure.

So when I turned seventeen and my father suggested that I go into the military, I didn't question him. I also didn't know much about politics; it wasn't part of my life. Now I understand how important it is to know what is going on in the world. Though no long-term solutions to our world's problems are achieved through political ideologies, I am impacted by them, as is each of us, and a dear price is paid because of this kind of ignorance.

Today I understand that my father and the men and women of his generation were filled with illusions and denial about how deeply they were affected by their military service and war experiences. Having come home as the victors, they were thrust into a role: They became the protectors of our culture's denial about the profound and far-reaching impact of war—not just on those who fought, but on all of us. This cultural myth obliged my father's generation not to talk openly or directly about the reality of the individual war experience, and in a sense, for many of them, their inner lives had to be abandoned. Speaking truthfully wasn't encouraged in them or in me. But something unusual happened during and after the war in Vietnam: Many of us could no longer deny reality.

I volunteered to go to Vietnam because I thought it was the right thing to do. I didn't understand the nature of war or the nature of violence. Three days after I was in-country I began to understand. It was insane. It's difficult to describe what I saw. I could and can still taste and smell it and see the emptiness in everyone's eyes. It was like being in a surreal horror movie.

I was sent to Vietnam "unattached," which means that I did not have a specific unit assignment. My orders sent me to the Ninetieth Replacement Battalion in Long Binh. Each morning those of us who were there would get up, make our beds, eat breakfast, and then stand in formation for roll call. We'd then count off by fives or threes or something like that. Some days all the ones would get an assignment and ship out, some days the twos, and so on. For those of us who did not get a unit assignment, there were details such as cleaning latrines, which entailed hauling a cut-down fifty-gallon drum from under the toilet seat and then burning the human waste that it contained, or working in the kitchen preparing meals, scrubbing pots, that sort of thing.

One of these details was to clean up some of the huge warehouses full of stuff for the PX (post exchange) system. The PX is the military version of a Wal-Mart, where soldiers can go to buy food, cigarettes, and so forth. As I had not yet received a unit assignment, I was put on this detail and, bizarrely, spent my first three days in Vietnam destroying thousands of pounds of Milky Way candy bars (which were melting and rotting in the tropical conditions). With the encouragement of a noncommissioned officer in charge, I also "confiscated" (military language for stole) a necklace of cultured Mikimoto pearls, a purchase item that was far beyond my wallet. Two days later I brought them back because I knew that stealing was just wrong. But this confused, corrupt, surreal world of the war was just an extension of my experiences in basic training, where I was formally schooled in the absurd and grotesque reality of violence.

During basic training I was taught to hate. On the firing range we were shooting at targets that resembled people. We were learning to kill *human beings*. We had to be taught how to do that—that is the work of the military. This work is done in a variety of subtle and not-so-subtle ways. When we were done on the firing range, we were supposed to stack our weapons in a particular way. One day, as I was preparing to place my rifle on the stack, I dropped it. The drill instructor, a sergeant first class, screamed and cursed that I wasn't looking after my rifle properly, that my rifle was the most important thing in my life, because whether I lived or died depended on it.

This guy was six feet three inches to my five feet eight and a half. He stood in front of me, his chest jammed up against my face, stabbing me with his finger and screaming obscenities down at me. Then he pulled out his penis and urinated on me, in front of everyone.

I wasn't allowed to wash for two days. I felt shame at such a deep level, I couldn't begin to handle it. Instead, all I felt was rage. I couldn't act it out on him because I would have gone to jail. So I focused my rage on *the enemy*. The enemy was everyone unlike me, everyone who was not an American soldier. This conditioning is an essential ingredient in the creation of a good soldier. Soldiers are trained to see anything other as dangerous, threatening, and potentially deadly. You dehumanize the enemy. You dehumanize yourself. My military training ultimately taught me to dehumanize a whole race of people. There was no distinction between the Vietcong, the regular Vietnamese army, and the Vietnamese general population.

But if I hadn't been prepared for this military training by the rest of my life, that kind of teaching wouldn't have taken hold. As a young man I was encouraged to fight, to be prejudiced and nationalistic. I was taught that the way to solve problems was through violence. If there was a conflict, the strongest person won. I learned this from my mother, my father, my teachers, and my friends.

At the age of five I was living with my parents in an apartment in Waterford, Pennsylvania, a small farming community in the northwestern part of the state. My father was a teacher, and my mother took in laundry, cleaned houses, and sometimes worked as a waitress or a barmaid to make ends meet. One day I wanted to ride my bicycle, and my mother didn't want me to. I was excited, and being a kid, I was persistent. My mother's response was to push me and my bicycle down a flight of stairs—twenty steps. Why I wasn't seriously injured, I don't know. Kids are flexible, perhaps. And they learn quickly.

This wasn't a one-time event. My mother often reacted with violence. One day, for no apparent reason, she placed her hand on the back of my neck, pulled me around, and smashed my face into a wall. Then she said to me that if only I were a better person, she wouldn't have to do that to me. I was being taught through these experiences to block out pain and to trust no one, especially those in authority.

My father was an emotionally hidden person. Most of the time alcohol, tobacco, and other intoxicants provided the bonding agent that held his walls of repression in place. But, as is always the case, repression does not really work as a strategy for dealing with strong emotions. Some of what's hidden squeezes out.

In the town where I lived, there was a lake, and in the springtime the water level would rise because of the snow-melt. One day when I was around eight I went out to play. I had been given a new pair of tennis shoes with a clean and distinctive tread. That day I was supposed to be home at four o'clock. But what does a child know about time? When I didn't come home at four, my father got concerned and went looking for me. He went down near the lake and found small footprints going into the water but not coming back. The footprints resembled the tread of my new pair of tennis shoes. He became terrified with the thought that I had fallen into the lake and drowned. He came rushing back, and when he got home, I was already there.

He immediately took me into the bathroom, pulled down my pants, took off his leather belt, and beat me until

I was black and blue and bleeding from the middle of my neck to my ankles. In the middle of what he was doing he realized that he was really hurting me, and he stopped beating me and started to doctor the wounds with Mercurochrome. As he was doing this, he said that he had beaten me because he loved me. All the time he was dressing my wounds, he kept repeating that he had done this to me because he loved me. That was the beginning of a long-term association: Love equals violence.

I don't believe that my father's intention was to hurt me. He just could not be afraid, could not stand to feel the reality of his powerlessness, so he expressed his fear through the only feeling he had access to: his anger. Unable to understand or tolerate the intensity of his emotions, he chose to see his problem as external. Then all he needed to do was control the perceived source of his distress. He was violent because he was not able to touch his own suffering. And therefore his suffering was acted out on me in this way. My mother was also unable to have honest access to her feelings, to look at her suffering, and her pain became violence toward me.

My father's denial and repression ultimately destroyed him: He died at the age of fifty-three from a lifestyle that was dominated by his alcoholism, his addiction to cigarettes (he smoked fifty nonfiltered cigarettes a day), and his general tendencies toward self-destruction. My father did not so much die as he was unable to live. I believe that the culture of denial destroyed him, as it destroyed his father and almost destroyed me. Yet this kind of denial is required to support the myth that war and violence are effective and lasting solutions to conflict.

The path to Vietnam

From an early age, I was taught that if I loved my country, I had to be ready to fight and die for it. When I went into military training, I volunteered to fight in Vietnam. They told me that I was going there to bring peace, that peace is accomplished at the point of a gun. And why would I have believed any different?

When I finished high school, I went directly into the military. I had been offered an athletic scholarship at a university, but my father urged me to turn the offer down because, he said, "You're not stable enough. You'll only go there and flunk out. You're too wild."

There was some truth in what he said. I was an unmanageable kid. If I were to do now some of the things that I was doing then, I'd probably get arrested and perhaps go to jail. It was just a different time. I used to steal cars regularly, just to drive them around. I would go down to the local Plymouth dealership and go through the used cars until I found one with a key in the ignition. I would start it up and drive it around all night on a joy ride and then return it. Nothing ever happened to me or to the cars. Lucky, I guess.

Without any parental supervision, I made my own rules. My father didn't seem able to provide any structure or guidance, as he was too busy drinking, too preoccupied with his own suffering. So I grew up pretty much on my own from the time I was about twelve years old.

I ended up joining the military because I didn't know what else to do. My father suggested it, and he was my father. Even an absent father remains a powerful figure in a family's life, particularly in a son's. He and his friends who fought in the Second World War would all sit around and get drunk and tell stories that made war seem glamorous, exciting, and romantic. I not only listened to these stories, I drank them in, longing to be a part of them.

So I believed the stories, without question, listened to my father, without question, and joined the army. But one doesn't need to grow up with a father who is an ex-soldier to hear romantic and misleading stories about war. Popular culture produces endless movies that romanticize and glorify war. They almost never portray the reality of this experience.

And war, whether real or in the movies, is not the only place where a warrior mentality is cultivated. It is also nurtured through sports. I was very talented in all the sports that were offered in school: baseball, football, and wrestling. The only thing that kept me in school was my athletic ability. And in every sport and on every team, I found this warrior mentality. I developed a romantic vision of what competition, fighting, and battle were like. I envisioned war as just another game.

At the same time, I was extremely insecure, shy, withdrawn, and untrusting. I had the notion that if I went into the military, fought in a war, and received a lot of medals, I would come home a hero, and I would be loved, admired, and cared for. That is how the stories went. It would just happen like that, and I wouldn't have to think about anything. "Go into the military," my father said, "it will help make a man out of you." And becoming a man, I thought, would mean being respected and being loved.

I remember the day I left for my military service. My father drove me to the bus station in Erie, Pennsylvania, a distance of about twenty-five miles from home. I had a little brown suitcase, a Boy Scout suitcase. My name was written on it in black Magic Marker. My father took me to the station, bought me a ticket, and left me. There was no good-bye hug, no handshake, no parting words. He just left me there to wait for the bus, and I went numb.

The bus took me from Erie to Buffalo, New York, ninety miles away, where I was going to be inducted. When I got to Buffalo, a man at the army induction center gave me a voucher to stay in a hotel. The first thing I did was to go out and buy some alcohol. I was terrified.

The next morning I was pretty sick, but I had to get up and go to the induction center. We all had to go through the physical, fill out a lot of papers. Then we went into a room and took an oath. I was a soldier.

The next day we went by train to Fort Dix, New Jersey. When we got off the bus that took us to the base, a staff sergeant greeted us by screaming obscenities at us, humiliating obscenities. Immediately I thought, "My father lied to me. I made the wrong choice." I just wanted to go home, but I couldn't. My life was about to be changed forever.

First we received our basic issue: uniforms, boots, underwear, blankets, towels, and a duffle bag. Then we had to get our hair cut. It was 1965, the beginning of the hippie era. My hair was quite long, even for then. The Beatles' influence. When I came up to the barber, everyone started calling me professor, I guess because of my long hair. I didn't have any understanding of what was going on. But I sat down in the chair and the barber shaved my head. It was humiliating.

The eight weeks of basic training were, in the beginning, a terrible struggle for me. I excelled at all the physical aspects of training, but I had a tremendously difficult time with what was being called discipline, because it didn't make any sense. We would have a barracks inspection: The company XO (executive officer, or assistant commander) would come in with white gloves, and if there was the slightest bit of dust anywhere, he would be propelled into a tirade, screaming obscenities at the top of his lungs. He would knock over wall lockers and our bunks, randomly dump footlockers on the floor and scatter the contents around the barracks. When he was finished he would give us twenty minutes to be ready for reinspection.

For no clear reason we would have to scrub the shower room floor with a toothbrush, or dry shave (without water or lubrication). We would be called out by a drunken drill sergeant at two in the morning with orders to stand formation in the freezing rain in our underwear, with our boots fully laced, our collar brass in one hand and our belt buckle in the other hand, all highly shined. The emotional, psychological, and spiritual cruelty of all this made no sense. What I didn't grasp then was that basic training was really about breaking me down. Breaking me down and building me up in the image that they wanted. I was resistant to this, so I had a very difficult time.

At one point, about midway through basic training, I was feeling so despondent and desperate that I came into the barracks and punched out every window in the place with my bare fists. My hands cut and bleeding, I went upstairs into a room, closed the door, pushed a wall locker in front of it, climbed out the window, and sat on the roof.

A first lieutenant, an aggressive, angry man in his early twenties, managed to get out to where I was on the roof. At this point I was crying and I didn't know what to do, I had so many feelings. His response was to slap me. He slapped my face and then punched me repeatedly. If I had reported what he did to me, he would have been in serious trouble. But it didn't occur to me that he shouldn't do that; abuse seemed normal to me by then.

Later a staff sergeant talked to me. He was a nice man, a good man, and he talked to me with what seemed at the time to be some measure of compassion. He seemed to genuinely care about me, and he ended up helping me to adjust to this world I found myself in. He said: "Listen to me. You're not going to go home, you're here for three years, so you might as well make the best of it."

There was something about the way he said it that made me just shut down to everything I was feeling. I said to myself, "Okay, I'll just do this thing, be the best soldier that I can be. I'll just turn off my feelings and do the best I can."

A part of me really wanted to get out. I just didn't know how to do it. Through all my military experience, in basic training and in Vietnam, I was the youngest around and completely at a loss.

As my training went on, I became increasingly troubled. Coming from a little country town, I had no skills to deal with the kind of people I was meeting. I was hustled a lot. I was used a lot, manipulated by other soldiers. My life became unmanageable, out of control. I was drinking a lot more by then, every chance I had.

Because of my heavy drinking, my paycheck would be gone long before the next one came. I was constantly in debt and in trouble with the people that I was borrowing money from. My life was in a tailspin, and yet there was a strange continuity with my childhood. The military was just a natural continuation of the abuse, neglect, and confusion that I had experienced all my life.

To escape my troubles, I volunteered for active duty in Vietnam. At first they said I couldn't go because I was too young. I persisted because I needed out of the mess of my life. Then I was told that I had to write an essay explaining why I wanted to go and if the essay was convincing enough, I would be granted the transfer. This was now 1966. The war was escalating, the fighting was heavy, casualties were heavier, and they needed more troops. I'm also sure that the unit I was stationed with was quite glad to get rid of me. Today I cannot remember what I wrote in that essay, but whatever it was, it worked.

During my tour in Vietnam I was directly responsible for the deaths of many, many people. But after the horrors of basic training, and after my childhood of abuse and neglect, I didn't recognize what I was doing as killing people. The enemy was simply the enemy, not human.

In combat

I had been in my first assignment, in Long Binh with the Ninetieth Replacement Battalion, for about ten days when I was randomly assigned to an assault helicopter company to be a door gunner. "Collect your things," I was told. "Here are your orders. Those people will take you where you're going." There was no time to think about it or to realize what was happening.

In Phu Loi, near Saigon, I was assigned to the 116th Assault Helicopter Company. I was taken to the barracks and given a bunk and a place to put my things, and then I was introduced to Richie, the crew chief I would fly with. He showed me where the gun shack was, where the tools of my new trade were kept: the M6o (7.62 mm) machine guns. He showed me how to clean the guns and took me out to the helicopter to demonstrate how to mount and load them.

He introduced me to the pilots and told me that we'd begin with a simple day, just flying pass runs and mail runs. I didn't have any idea what that meant; everything was new and I was scared to death. When we took off, my job was to tell the pilot we were clear on the right and to watch for approaching aircraft (I was the pilot's rearview mirror). I had no idea what I was doing, not a clue. I didn't even really understand that I could get shot. I felt scared and confused, and I knew that I was not supposed to be either.

We made several trips that day to different locations to pick up and deliver mail, and we took soldiers to Saigon on pass. The more we flew, the more familiar I became with things. The weather was great, the air was cool and dry, and I remember feeling a sense of wonder about this thing called war.

We were just finishing up our runs as night approached. We returned to Phu Loi, ate, and I went to my barrack and lied down on my bunk. I noticed that there weren't many people around, but I didn't think too much about it. Then Richie came running in and told me excitedly to get my things together, that the unit had gotten into a mess, some ships were down and we needed to fly. I got dressed, grabbed my flight gloves, flack jacket, flight helmet, and rushed down to the gun shack where I grabbed clean M6os and ran them out to the bunker where the helicopter was parked.

I mounted the guns and as I waited for the rest of the crew I saw that there was a lot of activity around some helicopters sitting on the flight line. When I walked closer I saw that men with water trucks were hosing blood out of the crew compartments. Richie grabbed me by the arm and told me to get to the helicopter because it was time to go. I climbed into the right-side crew compartment, put on my flight helmet, and plugged in my microphone cord. We did a radio check and then Richie gave the clear-left and I gave the clear-right announcement to the pilots. We hovered into the blackness above the airfield and took off.

Soon we arrived at a staging location where there were several other helicopters. This was my first experience flying with the whole unit. Troops were loaded into the helicopters and we took off again into the night. As we approached the landing zone (or LZ), the sky was lit up with parachute flares that gave the darkness a bright yellowish tint. Though you could see, everything seemed in silhouette. Forms were identifiable but not clearly. As we began to descend into the LZ, I sensed a tense and exciting energy in the air: the feeling of unspoken fear. The pilot gave the order to open fire. The next thing I knew we were on the ground and all of the troops were off the helicopter. Other ships were taking off all around us but we weren't. We had been shot down.

Richie yelled at me to get the pilot out and grab the guns. I ran to the pilot's door, opened it and unlocked a sliding piece of body armor (designed to protect the side of the pilot's head). We had been instructed to be cautious when sliding this piece back because we could easily push it right off its track and damage the floor of the helicopter. Well I did exactly what I was not supposed to and, wrapped up in my guilt, I didn't notice at first that the pilot had been shot. When I realized he was seriously wounded, I didn't know what to do. I ran for Richie. He told me to unbuckle the pilot and get him out of the ship if he wasn't able to get out himself. I had to pull the pilot out of his seat and over my shoulder because he was unconscious. I laid him down and then I grabbed my machine gun and then Richie's and laid them down next to the pilot. I didn't realize until the next morning that the pilot was dead.

Richie told me that the company would send in a helicopter to get us out. We ended up spending the entire night in the LZ. So my first day ended in heavy, heavy combat. Emotionally, I went numb. All around me, I saw, heard, and felt the wounded. I had been trained as an infantryman, trained in small arms and heavy weapons, trained in first aid. But all the training I had didn't prepare me for what happened when I found myself on the ground in heavy fighting. So I fell back on childhood experiences of playing cowboys and Indians, playing war, and I played well.

Soon there were one dead, two wounded. I was terrified, but I couldn't be. I didn't know whether to shoot or to be quiet. I decided to be quiet because I didn't really know what else to do. Once you expose your position, you're vulnerable. It was just like playing cowboys and Indians in the woods, except the bullets were real.

During all that time, waiting to be evacuated, I didn't cry. I didn't cry and I didn't pray. I would hear a lot of men, when they were really scared, cry for their mothers or somebody or pray. But I was proud of myself. "I'm not crying, I'm not praying. Because who would I pray to?" It didn't make sense to believe in God. If there was a God, how could this happen? Finally the intense fighting quieted and we were evacuated in the morning.

I went on to become a very good soldier. I received many awards and decorations. And I enjoyed my job! Not in the way you might enjoy a hike in the mountains, but I enjoyed it in the sense that I felt useful and I could function well there. Imagine that, the chaos of war, the insanity of war—this was where I felt comfortable.

That vulnerable boy, eighteen years old, scared to death. Gone! Gone! Gone! Just like that, the first action, shot down—gone. There was no place for that boy, no room for those kinds of feelings. You can't have access to your feelings and function in such a situation.

In Vietnam I wasn't fighting for democracy or any ideals. That myth died within the first couple of weeks. What was left then was just to be the best soldier I could be so I could help myself, and as many of the other soldiers as possible, stay alive. That became the reality of serving.

Later I was promoted to the position of crew chief on helicopters. I crewed slick ships (the helicopters that carried soldiers into battle, did medical evacuations and resupplies) and gunships (helicopters that were used to provide close fire support for the soldiers on the ground). From the point at which I became a crew chief, nearly every day that I was in Vietnam I was in combat. One of the many decorations I received was the Air Medal. To get an air medal, you must fly twenty-five combat missions and twenty-five combat hours. By the end of my tour, I had been awarded more than twenty-five air medals. That amounts to somewhere in the neighborhood of 625 combat hours and combat missions. All of those combat missions killed people, but I never saw them as people.

The only experience I had with the Vietnamese people was that they were my enemy. Every one of them: shopkeepers, farmers, women, children, babies. Once we were shut down (parked) outside a village in the Mekong Delta area. For some reason, a group of six other soldiers and I went into the village. It was in an area where a lot of hostile action was taking place, but this village was supposed to be pacified, friendly. When we walked into the village, we passed three or four men who appeared to be Buddhist monks: They all had shaved heads and saffron robes. When they were about thirty or forty meters beyond us, they turned and opened fire on us with AK-47s. Of the seven of us, three were killed and two were wounded. Killed and wounded by monks. Were they really monks? I don't know. They looked like monks to us. So monks were our enemy too.

On another occasion the infantry unit that our company supported began to receive heavy automatic weapons fire from a village, so they radioed us and asked for help. We flew in with a heavy-fire team (three B-model Huey gunships with rockets and 7.62 mm machine guns, one with a 40 mm cannon), opened fire, and without thought destroyed the entire village. We destroyed everything. The killing was complete madness. There was nothing there that was not the enemy. We killed everything that moved: men, women, children, water buffalo, dogs, chickens. Without any feeling, without any thought. Simply out of this madness. We destroyed buildings, trees, wagons, baskets, everything. All that remained when we were finished were dead bodies, fire, and smoke. It was all like a dream; it didn't feel real. Yet every act that I was committing was very real.

My job in Vietnam was to kill people. By the time I was first injured in combat (two or three months into my tour), I had already been directly responsible for the deaths of several hundred people. And today, each day, I can still see many of their faces.

ॐ

There is much of my war experience that escapes my memory. Days blended one into the next; time was marked by the heat of the day and the disappearance of light, although the disappearance of light could as easily mark death. At one point I was involved in a special operations mission somewhere near the Duc Hua rubber plantation, which was on the Saigon River about a one-hour flight north of Saigon, where the river served as a border with Cambodia. I hated flying in this area. I had been shot down twice in this vicinity and shot up numerous other times. This place was too dangerous.

This time we were sent to pick up a group of *chu hoi*, Vietcong soldiers who had surrendered. On our way to this location, the call came in over the radio that some of these men had changed their minds and run. We were already in the air, so we made contact with our ground forces and were directed to the area where the *chu hoi* were thought to be. Flying just above treetop, we spotted what we believed to be them and flew down, herding these men like cattle to a rice paddy dike. We hovered next to them, with the plan that the gunner and I would get out of the helicopter, bind them, put them in the helicopter, and return to the base of operations.

As we hovered there the *chu hoi* were waving their arms above their heads in a gesture of surrender. We had them at gunpoint, and just as I was about to jump out of the ship, one of them threw something into the helicopter. Someone on the ship yelled "Grenade!" and we instantly opened fire. I began frantically looking for the thing, to throw it out, not recognizing that it should already have exploded, so it must have been a dud. At the same time, the pilot began flailing the helicopter about wildly in a reflex to get rid of it. I managed to find the grenade, reported it as a dud, and instead of throwing it out of the ship, I just held it for a time. (I ended up holding on to it for some hours, unscrewing and removing the firing pin then screwing it back in, until someone suggested that it might be best to get rid of it.)

Once the chaos settled, we stayed there for a while and looked on as the man who had thrown the grenade slowly died from his wounds. The burst from the M60 machine gun had all but cut him in half, and he was lying there with his intestines hanging out of his body, still waving his hands in a gesture of surrender. We hovered there and just watched him die.

I flew on a similar operation right before my tour ended. We were again sent near the Duc Hua rubber plantation, this time to pick up a group of "Kit Carson Scouts," Vietcong soldiers who had surrendered and then agreed to work for us as double agents. They were used to infiltrate enemy groups of all types; they would then desert and be picked up by U.S. forces at a prescribed place and time to report what they had learned. These operations gave me the creeps because the whole concept seemed so bizarre to me. How could these men be trusted?

This time, as we approached our pickup point, we hovered at the side of a tree line. Suddenly there was a loud sound, and I knew it was not good. In my peripheral vision I saw that the helicopter next to ours was upside down and burning.

Events unfolded quickly, and somehow it seemed as if this hadn't just happened but had always been. The space around us filled with the orange-red glow of tracer rounds crackling like storm-downed electric wires. I could feel the rounds hitting the ship—thump . . . thump, thump, thump. Our pilots immediately lifted the tail of the helicopter, pointing the nose down, and rotated back and forth in a 180-degree arc as we opened up with all of the firepower we had. We positioned ourselves between the incoming fire and the downed ship as best we could, spinning and whirling, digging into our airspace, acting like a giant mechanical badger protecting its den.

The Special Forces sergeant who was riding with us went into a panic and started yelling, "Get out, get out of here, get out!"

I remember turning my focus toward him while I continued to fire, yelling at him at the top of my lungs to shut up and shoot. I fired my M60 machine gun until the barrel glowed red. I stopped firing for an instant, changed the barrel, then began firing again. The pilot maneuvered our helicopter around and behind the downed ship, and I jumped out to assist the crew on board. Amazingly, they had all survived.

We beat it back to the rubber plantation, dropped off the boys, and flew back to our main base, Cu Chi, where our company maintenance facility was located. We could not operate this helicopter any longer. It was leaking fuel and hydraulics; it was out of action. We knew we were shot up, we just didn't know how badly. We really didn't want to know, didn't really care. Indifference and terror were completely intermingled.

We flew over to the maintenance area, landed, went through the usual procedures of shutting down. Then I headed up to the hooch (barracks) to pack up my stuff because I was supposed to be leaving the country at 0800 hours the next morning. It seemed I had survived my tour of duty and it was time to rotate back to the States.

I packed up, had some beers, went to sleep, woke up, ate breakfast, and headed out to the airstrip for my last helicopter ride in Vietnam. This one took me to Bien Hoa Air Base to begin my trip home. When we landed, I grabbed my stuff and started to walk away from the helicopter. I turned around to wave good-bye or something, but the helicopter was already hovering to a position for takeoff, so I just walked over to a Quonset hut with my orders. In a blink I was walking up a set of portable steps to board a jumbo jet to the States.

During the flight back I didn't talk to anyone. I had absolutely nothing to say. It was as if my mind were frozen, held in stasis or something. Besides, conversation, unless functional, was simply not important. I didn't really want to bother with getting to know anyone because then when they rotated or were wounded or killed there was no connection to lose, no person to lose. This was the style while in Vietnam, and flying back I had even less reason to talk to anyone.

The flight went from Bien Hoa to Tokyo to Anchorage to Travis Air Force Base in California. Because we crossed the international date line, we arrived the same day that we had left. We deplaned and boarded buses with blackened windows so that we would not be exposed to the protesters who were waiting outside the gate with their antiwar signs, their slogans, their hatred directed toward us.

The other war

We were transported to Oakland Army Depot, and as hard as I try to remember, there just aren't any memories between being there and finding myself in the Newark airport, where I had to change planes to fly to Erie, Pennsylvania. I vividly remember walking through the airport in uniform with all my ribbons, insignias, unit patches, flight wings, and so forth. When I reflect on this period, it seems so surreal that in just forty-eight hours I went from intense combat to walking across Newark airport to board a plane for home.

As I was making my way through the airport, I noticed a beautiful young girl across the transit hall, and she was looking directly at me. You know what I mean. You can be in a room with a thousand people, and when someone is looking at you, you know it. As I began walking down the hallway, she began to walk toward me, and as we came closer to one another, I could see her more clearly. This was 1968, with hippies everywhere and that particular style of dress, that look. She had long auburn hair, straight and shiny, parted in the middle. She had the most beautiful brown eyes and full lips. She was wearing a long, loose-fitting dress. I think it was tan with a brightly colored flower print. The dress went down to her ankles and was cut relatively low in the front, allowing me to see just the hint of her breasts, soft, inviting, intimidating. She also wore a thin piece of leather as a necklace, with a pendant hanging from it. This pendant nestled delicately in the soft hollow at the base of her throat.

As she approached, I knew what she wanted. I knew from all of the films that I had seen, from all the stories that

I had heard from my father and the others who had come home from the Second World War. She was coming to greet me, to thank me. She would come to me, throw her arms around me, and kiss me deeply. As we came closer and closer together, my excitement and my anxiety grew. Would I measure up to her expectations?

While these thoughts were running through my mind, I was not paying attention to my progress across the hall. The next thing I knew, I was looking down at her feet exactly in front of me. Beautiful feet, delicate toes held so softly in leather sandals, the laces of which disappeared under her dress. I lifted my head up, exhaled, and with great expectation prepared myself for my hero's welcome. As our eyes met, with one deft movement, she spit on me.

I stood there stunned, frozen in place. Before I could begin to move again, she simply turned and walked away.

I was flooded with feelings and impulses, the strongest of which was to annihilate the enemy. Since she had committed an act of violence against me, she was the enemy. Why I didn't kill her on the spot I still don't know. Desperately confused and in unbearable, inaccessible pain, all I could do was go to the nearest bar and get drunk. I then went directly to the men's room, took off my uniform, and put on civilian clothes. I didn't have any clear, conscious thought about it. I just did it.

When I got home from the war I had a short leave and then reported to Ireland Army Hospital at Fort Knox, Kentucky. I was there to have my shoulder repaired because it had been seriously damaged in a helicopter accident in the summer of 1967. (On our way to a combat mission the front of our skids had gotten caught in a rice paddy dike, causing the helicopter to flip over and throwing me hard against the pilot's seat.) My shoulder had been repaired as best as possible in-country, and my injury had not been deemed severe enough to send me home. After returning to the States at the end of my tour, I spent the next nine months in the hospital and in physical therapy.

As my date of discharge from the hospital approached, I was told that my medical treatment was not yet complete and that I should agree to become what's called a "medical holdover." What I understood about this proposition was that I would then become the property of the military until they thought that I was well enough to be discharged. Because I had developed a profound distrust of the intentions of the military (and the government as a whole), I would not agree. I was then informed that in order to be released from the hospital, I had to sign a waiver of medical responsibility. What wasn't explained to me was that by signing this waiver, I was releasing the government from any responsibility in my ongoing medical care. I could make no claim of disability and would not be compensated for the wounds that I received while serving in Vietnam. (Another hustle, another cheap trick.) After signing the medical waiver, I was released from the hospital and discharged from the army almost simultaneously.

When I got out of the hospital, I found myself unable to socialize or reintegrate back into my own culture. I felt so very different, and the people at home were not interested in helping me and other soldiers like me to reenter society. We were kept at a distance, emotionally, psychologically, even physically. We were very distinctly marginalized. I understood this, felt it deeply, but I didn't know how to deal with it.

At the time, the war was ever-present in my thoughts. Everything I touched reminded me of it. I was unable to sleep. When I tried to talk to people about the war, they would just say to me, "All that's over now, you should forget it. You survived. Get on with your life." But I wasn't able to do that. So I started using drugs to cover my pain and loneliness; to cover my rejection; to dull the memories; to hide from the sounds, the faces, the smells that clung to me like skunk spray.

When I came back from Vietnam I wanted to be like I was before I went to war. I wanted to be seventeen years old again and live a normal life. It wasn't possible. I no longer fit in. I had been trained to be a killer and never helped to become something other than a killer. I was just turned loose, left to my own devices.

While I was in the hospital, I had a medical leave and went back to my hometown, with my upper body in a cast. While at home I went to a football game. I was standing near one of the goals, watching the game, when someone lit a firecracker. My immediate reaction was to dive to the ground. The people standing around me all laughed. Because my body was in a cast from my waist to my neck, I struggled to get up. Finally on my feet, in panic and embarrassment, I started to run. But it was the laughter. This laughter was more painful than the bullets. I ran and I ran and I ran, trying to run away from my feelings, run to safety. I didn't stop running until 1983.

My running took many different forms. I ran by using drugs, alcohol, cigarettes, sex, by moving from place to place. I never lived in one place for more than six months because I could not stand to have anyone get close to me, get to know me, because I thought that if anyone really knew me, they would hate me. And the message was clear; it was given to me daily: Because I was a soldier from Vietnam, I was not worth anything.

There was no "after the war" for me. My life, as a survivor of Vietnam, was an ongoing war. I isolated myself more and more from other people, took more and more drugs, and lived more and more on the fringes of society.

During all this time, I was always looking outside myself for some salvation, for some kind of answer. If I could do the right combination of drugs, the feelings would go away. Or if I could have the right job, I would be okay.

After I was released from the hospital, in August of 1968, I returned to Pennsylvania, started college, and married my high school sweetheart. But I was incapable of intimacy, and the marriage did not last. While attending college, I had many relationships, none of which lasted. I don't know if I had any real intention that they last, but somewhere in my mind I kept telling myself before each encounter that this was the one. I felt what I interpreted as a powerful connection, and that could only mean that physical union was the answer to my problems. We would have sex, then my deadness would return, and I would abandon that woman in search of the next.

At the beginning of college I was a physical education major. Sports having been my saving grace in high school, I thought that I wanted to be a physical education teacher and a coach. As part of this curriculum, I had to take practicum classes, one of which was social dance. In this class I met a young woman from McKeesport, Pennsylvania. She was an athlete, a diver on the swim team. She was shy, quiet, and she had grown up with a mother that was very religious and protective. She became my dance partner, and those feelings came again, so I pursued her.

I don't remember when we first consummated the relationship or how long it continued, but one day I was talking to her on the phone and she told me that she was pregnant. I don't remember exactly how I felt in that moment. There were real struggles with what to do next, but being a stand-up guy, I felt the only real solution was marriage. This was a time when abortion was becoming more of an option, but I just knew that I couldn't do that, and for me this decision had everything to do with Vietnam. I didn't really want to get married, but I did want to have the child. I believed with all my being that this child would somehow be my salvation, that having this child would be the ingredient that would give my life purpose, my life being completely devoid of meaning, feeling, and connection.

We had a son. When he was a small baby, he slept in a bassinet in the bedroom with his mother and me. When my baby son cried, I became intensely agitated, so much so that I would have to get high or leave the house. I didn't understand why, I just had to get away. I thought I was insane, crazy, that there was something wrong with me. Whenever he cried, I would feel the need to leave, to run. I realize now that there were multiple reasons for my intense reactions to his crying. For one thing, crying, my own or anyone else's, terrified me, was intolerable to me. Sadness had always been a forbidden emotion. But there were also other reasons why his crying caused me to panic, reasons that I wasn't yet ready to acknowledge and wouldn't confront for years to come. But by the time my son was three years old, I felt I couldn't stay there any longer. I left him

and his mother. I was completely controlled by my suffering and unaware of how deeply afraid I was of facing what
was inside me. I just knew that I couldn't stay still.

After the war I was asked to participate in the peace movement, and I did participate. But I was very clear that I was
not a pacifist. I participated because I believed the war
should end, but only because it wasn't being fought properly. If we were going to be in Vietnam, then we should
fight to win. If we weren't going to fight to win, then we
shouldn't be there. That's how I felt in 1968, 1969.

Also, in my experience of this time, the peace movement was another war movement; it was often violent and
ugly. We Vietnam veterans were a prized possession, yet ex-
pendable at the same time. If we could serve the purpose of
the movement, then we were wanted, but when it came to
our healing, seldom was there any interest in helping us.

In 1969 or 1970 I went to Washington, D.C., with
other soldiers who had fought in Vietnam. We handcuffed
ourselves to the fence around the White House and took
our war medals and threw them over the fence. The police
came and beat us. This is the insanity of war, of violence.
These were the very same people I had fought for. These
were the people for whom I offered up my life.

In 1969 I was still in college in Pennsylvania. I think I
was the only combat veteran in my school at that time.
When the My Lai massacre occurred, I was taking a political science class. A discussion started about this massacre,
and people were talking about the horrific atrocity the
American soldiers had committed. These same students
self-righteously proclaimed that Lieutenant William Cal-
ley, who was responsible for this group of men, should die

for his actions. These were people of "peace"—the peace activists at this college, not soldiers—who talked like this.

I stood up in the class and said, "If this lieutenant is a war criminal, what about Harry Truman? He killed hundreds of thousands of Japanese civilians by giving the orders for the dropping of two bombs."

But they didn't want to address that. They only said: "Who are you to say this? You don't understand the nature of war."

It was at this point that I identified myself as a Vietnam combat veteran, disabled from that war, injured on several occasions and severely wounded, all before my nineteenth birthday. I said: "It's you who don't understand the nature of war. You don't understand what soldiers have to confront on a daily basis, have to confront just to protect your right to do what you are doing now. *You* don't understand."

I became overwhelmed with rage. Rage is different from anger. Rage is a huge, explosive ball of unaddressed feelings. Rage is the result of a deep sense of sadness, powerlessness, despair, and rejection. But I didn't know how to begin to relate to those feelings; I could only express them as rage. The next thing I knew, the police were escorting me out of the classroom at gunpoint.

From the time I came home from Vietnam until about a month before I went into a drug and alcohol rehabilitation program in 1983, I carried a gun everywhere. I couldn't feel safe without a gun. I slept with one, I ate with one, I went to school with one, I had one in my car. My sense of safety was completely dependent on this gun. I didn't yet understand that security and safety don't actually come from controlling the world around us (or within us). Later, from my study of the Buddhist teachings, I would learn that true and lasting security can come only from learning to live in harmony with our suffering.

One night in 1978 I found myself sitting on the steps of my house with an unloaded shotgun under my chin, pulling the trigger—click, click, click—screaming and crying, because my pain was so overwhelming. All I wanted was to die—but at the same time, I didn't really want to die, I just didn't know how to live with all this pain. I kept looking outside myself for something to help me, to fix me, to make it better. But nothing was working.

Many times I felt that the men who died in Vietnam were the lucky ones. Those of us who didn't die, who have had to live with the trauma and reality of this experience, continued to pay the price. We were the scapegoats for an entire country, for an entire culture that didn't want to take responsibility for its decisions and actions.

War does not begin with a declaration or end with an armistice. The seeds of war are constantly planted and the harvest is never-ending. I experienced the war before the war in my family, then the Vietnam war, and then the war after the war.

In 1985 I went to Washington, D.C., to see the Vietnam Veterans Memorial, a black stone wall with the names of the more than 58,000 Americans who died in Vietnam carved on it. (As of this writing, the number of Americans killed in Vietnam totals 58,206.) Though the wall went up in 1982, it took me another three years before I was able to go look at those names. The American involvement in Vietnam officially ended in 1975. Since 1975 until the time of this writing, it is estimated that more than 100,000 American men and women who served

in Vietnam have committed suicide. Approximately 40 to
60 percent of the homeless population in the United
States are Vietnam veterans. Vietnam veterans also have a
divorce rate that is much higher than national averages.
Like me, other veterans have lost the ability to have intimate relationships.

So you see that the war is not over; it never ends. My involvement in this war has scarred me in many ways. It
scarred my body, it scarred my heart, it scarred my soul.
The reality of this war lives with me today. It doesn't go
away. There is no sense in trying to hide it, because war
does not go away.

Vietnam was the first war after which society could not
sweep its soldiers' pain and anguish under the carpet of
heroism and adulation. The defeat and shame of that war
have allowed us to see more truthfully the defeat and shame
of all war and all violence, but Vietnam veterans have paid
a heavy price for this truthfulness.

The embrace of family and friends and the celebration
of ticker tape parades can seem to justify much hardship
and cruelty. But as I have been able to interact more and
more with people of my father's generation, I have discovered just how many veterans from the Second World War
spent their entire lives isolated from their families, suffering in silence. They have spent endless hours in the garage
or the basement alone, many of them—like my father and
other veterans that I grew up with—attempting to drink
away the guilt, the shame, the confusion, the fear, the
anger, all the feelings or lack of feelings that are the reality
of war. These men are trapped in a code of silence, and many
of them are dying there.

The military teaches you to dehumanize, but much in our society also teaches us to dehumanize. And once you dehumanize, once that becomes a habit, it doesn't change easily. When we dehumanize others, we lose our own humanity. This doesn't happen just in the military: It happens through television, in the movies, in magazines; it happens on the street; it happens in stores and in the workplace. Those who haven't served in the military are confronted with very similar kinds of issues. Think of the shootings in schoolyards, people beating someone to death because the person is gay, road rage. Even just shouting at someone in a checkout line because we can't tolerate the uncomfortable feelings that can arise when we have to wait. In many life experiences, we are dehumanizing others and being dehumanized.

The war in Vietnam, the war in the Persian Gulf, the war in Kosovo, the war on the streets of Los Angeles, Hartford, Denver, Cleveland, or any town, the wars that take place in our homes—what are the seeds of those wars? Vietnam is only an expression of something that begins inside each and every one of us, male or female. We all possess the seeds of violence, the seeds of war.

When I entered a rehabilitation center for drug addiction in 1983, I was able to stop using drugs, stop drinking. After I stopped using drugs and alcohol, the obvious intoxicants, I began to be able to learn what the other intoxicants were that were preventing me from looking at myself. And I began to stop those things also. I stopped using caffeine, I stopped using nicotine, I stopped eating processed sugar, I stopped eating meat, I stopped going from one relationship to another. I kept coming more and more back to myself, in my commitment to heal, even though I did not understand (in any intellectual way) what it was I was doing.

In 1990 it became impossible for me to hide from the reality of my Vietnam experience any longer. Vietnam was not just in my head; it was all through me. I had talked intellectually about Vietnam, but I had never fully opened myself to the totality of this experience. Now the pain reached a point where it was so great that I wanted only to hide from it, to run from it yet again. My first thought, of course, was to get drunk. When I drink, it covers the pain like a blanket. But under the blanket, inside me, is full of barbed wire; every time I move, it cuts at me, tears my skin. When I drink, I have the illusion that I have put a buffer between my skin and the barbed wire, but this is not the truth; when I am anesthetized, I am just not so aware of the ripping and tearing.

Well, this time I didn't have that drink. Instead I ended up at a Buddhist meditation retreat for Vietnam veterans led by the Vietnamese Zen master Thich Nhat Hanh.

2

The Light at the Tip of the Candle

Picture a candle burning. The flame at the tip is hot and bright, sending light into the darkness. This image supported me as I walked through the darkness of my life, the necessary path to waking up, to turning things around.

By 1990 I had abstained from drugs and alcohol for seven years. Now there were fewer places to hide from the reality of Vietnam. All my feelings about the war had been tightly repressed until then, and now they were coming to the surface. I couldn't push them away any longer.

At this time I was living in Concord, Massachusetts, and I was in counseling with a social worker, a wonderful, generous woman. When I got to the point where I felt totally overwhelmed by my emotions and wanted to die, she supported me, and in a spiritual way, she held me. I was trapped in the prison of self, confined by guilt, remorse, anxiety, and fear. I became so tormented that I was unable to leave my house. Physically and emotionally, I was under siege, bunkered in. My counselor continued to phone me and gently yet persistently invite me to come to her office.

She continued to support the reality that I had *not* gone completely mad and helped me to understand that what was happening to me was the result of getting in touch with my feelings about the war, perhaps for the first time.

At a certain point she told me about a Buddhist monk who had worked with Vietnam veterans and had some success in helping them become more at peace with themselves. She suggested I read some of his books. It was only later that she told me he was Vietnamese. Because I had committed myself to healing, I said: "Sure, okay, I'll read the books," but I wasn't able to, because they were written by a Vietnamese man—the enemy. Every time I would envision reading them, I would think about the monks who opened fire on us.

Six months later someone else, a woman in a therapy group I had joined, gave me a catalog from the Omega Institute, a holistic education center in Rhinebeck, New York. One of the pages of this catalog was bookmarked for me. When I opened it I saw a photo of that very same Vietnamese Buddhist monk, Thich Nhat Hanh, and an announcement that he was leading a meditation retreat for Vietnam veterans. Up to that point I had an excellent excuse for not going to see him: He lived in France and I didn't have the money to travel because I was unable to work; I was unemployable. There was a note in the catalog, highlighted for me in yellow, saying that scholarships were available for those in need. I couldn't use the excuse of not having any money. I had made the commitment that I was willing to go to any length to heal, so I had to take this step.

I called to make arrangements to go to the retreat. I explained to the person on the phone that I had a very difficult time being around people. I became anxious and uncomfortable in ordinary social circumstances and needed to be by myself. I also informed her that I had a very hard time sleeping at night, a polite way of indicating my intensely disturbed sleep pattern. The people at the Omega Institute were nervous about having me, one of those so-called unstable Vietnam vets, attend this retreat, so they called the organizers and asked if it was all right for me to participate. The sponsors said, "We don't turn anyone away." This was the response of the Vietnamese— my enemy. *They* said: "We don't turn anybody away." My countrymen, the people I fought for, wanted to reject me, yet again.

I drove to the retreat on my motorcycle. At that time I was riding a black Harley Davidson. I was dressed in a typical fashion for me: black leather jacket, black boots, black helmet, gold mirror glasses, and a red bandanna tied around my neck. My style of dress was not exactly warm and welcoming. The way I presented myself was intended to keep people away, because I was scared, really scared.

I arrived at the retreat early so I could check the place out. Before I could think about anything, I walked the perimeter of the whole place: Where are the boundaries? Where are the dangerous places where I'm vulnerable to attack? Coming here thrust me into the unknown, and for me the unknown meant war. And to be with so many people I didn't know was terrifying to me, and the feeling of terror also meant war.

After my recon I went down to the registration desk and asked where the camping area was, because I didn't want to camp where anyone else was camping. I was much too frightened to be near so many strangers. This time each day, sunset, was filled with fear—fear of ambush, fear of attack, fear of war exploding at any moment. Rationally I knew that these things wouldn't happen, but these fears, like the reality of war, are not rational.

I put my tent in the woods, away from everybody else, and I sat there asking myself, "What am I doing here? Why am I at a Buddhist retreat with a Vietnamese monk? I have to be out of my mind, absolutely crazy."

The first night of the retreat, Thich Nhat Hanh talked to us. The moment he walked into the room and I looked into his face, I began to cry. I realized for the first time that I didn't know the Vietnamese in any other way than as my enemy, and this man wasn't my enemy. It wasn't a conscious thought; it was an awareness happening from somewhere deep inside me.

As I sat there looking at this Vietnamese man, memories of the war started flooding over me. Things that I hadn't remembered before, events I had totally forgotten. One of the memories that came back that evening helped me to understand why I had not been able to tolerate the crying of my baby son years earlier.

At some point, maybe six months into my service in Vietnam, we landed outside a village and shut down the engines of our helicopters. Often when we shut down near a village the children would rush up and flock around the helicopter, begging for food, trying to sell us bananas or pineapples or Coca-Cola, or attempting to prostitute their mothers or sisters. On this particular day there was a large group of children, maybe twenty-five. They were mostly gathered around the helicopter. As the number of children grew, the situation became less and less safe because often the Vietcong would use children as weapons against us. So someone chased them off by firing a burst from an M60 machine gun over their heads. As they ran away, a baby was left lying on the ground, crying, maybe two feet from the helicopter in the middle of the group. I started to approach the baby along with three or four other soldiers. That is what my nonwar conditioning told me to do. But in this instance, for some reason, something felt wrong to me. And just as the thought began to rise in my head to yell at the others to stop, just before that thought could be passed by synapse to speech, one of them reached out and picked up the baby, and it blew up. Perhaps the baby had been a booby-trap, a bomb. Perhaps there had been a grenade attack or a mortar attack at just this moment. Whatever the cause, there was an explosion that killed three soldiers and knocked me down, covering me with blood and body parts.

This incident had been so overwhelming that my conscious mind could not hold it. And so this memory had remained inaccessible to me until that evening in 1990. As I sat there looking at this monk, Vietnam just came rushing back to me. All the unaddressed, repressed thoughts, feelings, and perceptions. I understood for the first time how the war had taken away my ability to have relationships. How the effects of war had prevented me, like my father before me, from having an intimate relationship with my son, or with anyone. I had left my three-year-old son and his mother not because I couldn't stand to be with them, which is what my suffering was telling me, but because I couldn't stand to be in my own skin.

Being in the presence of this monk and his assistant, a nun who was also Vietnamese, memories of the war continued to rush through me, and I was terrified all over again. In one instance, people from the retreat were standing in a circle, doing some exercises. I wouldn't join the circle because it didn't feel safe. When Sister Chan Khong began to walk away from the circle, I started to panic because I didn't have a gun. I was confronted by the memory of walking into that "pacified" village and the monks opening fire on us with their automatic weapons. And now here I was observing a Vietnamese nun leaving a group of American veterans who were unarmed and vulnerable. I was so frightened I thought that I might explode. Who could be trusted? Who?

At the retreat, Thich Nhat Hanh said to us, "You veterans are the light at the tip of the candle. You burn hot and bright. You understand deeply the nature of suffering." He told us that the only way to heal, to transform suffering, is to stand face-to-face with suffering, to realize the intimate details of suffering and how our life in the present is affected by it. He encouraged us to talk about our experiences and told us that we deserved to be listened to, deserved to be understood. He said we represented a powerful force for healing in the world.

He also told us that the nonveterans were more responsible for the war than the veterans. That because of the interconnectedness of all things, there is no escape from responsibility. That those who think they aren't responsible are the most responsible. The very lifestyle of the nonveterans supports the institutions of war. The nonveterans, he said, needed to sit down with the veterans and listen, really listen to our experience. They needed to embrace whatever feelings arose in them when engaging with us— not to hide from their experience in our presence, not to try to control it, but just to be present with us.

I spent six days at the retreat. Being with the Vietnamese people gave me the opportunity to step into the emotional chaos that was my experience of Vietnam. And I came to realize that this experience was—and continues to be—a very useful and powerful gift. Without specific awareness of the intimate nature of our suffering, whatever that suffering may be, healing and transformation simply are not possible and we will continue to re-create that suffering and infect others with it.

Toward the end of the retreat I went to Sister Chan Khong to apologize, to try to make amends in some way for all the destruction, the killing I'd taken part in. I didn't know how to apologize directly; perhaps I didn't have the courage. All I could manage to say was: "I want to go to Vietnam." During the retreat they had said, if we who had fought wanted to go to Vietnam to help rebuild the country, they would help arrange it. And so I asked to go to Vietnam; it was all I could say through my tears.

Sister Chan Khong looked at me as I was crying and said: "Before you go to Vietnam, perhaps it would be a good idea to come to Plum Village," which is Thich Nhat Hanh's monastery and retreat center in France. She said, "If you come in the summer, many Vietnamese people are there—refugees, boat people—and you can learn to know the Vietnamese in another way. Come to Plum Village; we can help you; let us help you!" I was overwhelmed by this offer of help. No one in my own country had made such an offer to me, an offer of support and help to live differently, to find peace.

At a very deep and profound level I understood the truth and sincerity of the offer. But the fact that it was being made by my enemy was both profound and confusing. In war it is impossible to distinguish safe from unsafe, good from bad. It is quite like the confusion of an abused child: All adults become potential abusers, even those who sincerely want to help. Violence and war contaminate daily life and personal interactions, permeating them with fear and distrust.

I replied to Sister Chan Khong's offer with deep gratitude and with hesitation. I said, "I'd like very much to come, but I can't. I don't have the money." And she answered, "Don't worry about the money." My travel expenses ended up being paid for with donations from the people who attended the retreat, and my stay in the monastery was supported by the Vietnamese community at Plum Village. My enemy embraced me and helped me in ways that my own country never did.

As soon as I agreed to go to the monastery in France, I felt a sense of lightness. A great weight lifted. I was excited and deeply touched by the act of caring and support offered to me by the Vietnamese. A couple of days later, however, I was again overcome by fear. In this country no one had ever reached out, offered help, without wanting to use me in some way. Why should I believe that my enemy, of all people, would help me, would embrace me like this? My fear said, "The only reason they are inviting me is that they want to put me on trial and then put me in jail or execute me for war crimes." My rational mind said, "I don't think this is the truth." But the fear was too deep to resist.

I knew that what I needed to do was to embrace my fear, look deeply into the nature of it, and go to France anyway. I promised myself I would go. "If they are going to kill me," I thought, "if that's what's going to happen, maybe at last I will have some peace."

That first summer at the monastery I stayed for six weeks. The community at Plum Village included about four hundred Vietnamese people. Everywhere I turned brought up another memory for me, brought me more and more in touch with the reality of the war—with the suffering I had witnessed, the despair I had felt, the trauma all of us on both sides had experienced. Everyplace, it was everyplace.

In Plum Village there are two separate living areas: a lower hamlet and an upper hamlet. The upper hamlet is where the Western people live; the lower hamlet is almost all Vietnamese people. When I arrived, there was a discussion about where I would stay. I thought I would probably live with the Westerners, but Sister Chan Khong said, "No, you will live with the Vietnamese." I wasn't able to do that exactly, to live within and among the Vietnamese. So I went to a place in the woods, maybe a quarter of a mile away from the community, and put up a tent. I set a perimeter around my tent of about twenty to thirty meters, and I put up booby traps—not to hurt anyone seriously, more to let me know that someone was there and to frighten them away.

Ten days before I left Plum Village, I took the booby traps down. I went to talk to Sister Chan Khong, and I told her about the booby traps. I explained that I hadn't wanted to hurt anyone; I just wanted to protect myself. She said to me, "It's good that you can take them down, but if you need to put them back up, put them back up." This was a kind of unconditional acceptance that I had never experienced.

What the Vietnamese community did is love me. They didn't put me on trial. They offered me an opportunity to look deeply into the nature of my self, to walk with them in mindfulness and begin the process of healing and transformation. It wasn't anything in particular that they said to me; it was simply being in community with Vietnamese people. Each face I saw brought another memory. The smell of food cooking brought memories; watching the celebrations brought memories. I saw the young women in their beautiful clothes, their *ao dais*, and I could hear the sound of war—automatic weapons fire, rockets, explosions, screaming—and smell gunpowder, blood, and death, and I remembered all the attacks on the villages that I had witnessed and participated in.

I couldn't talk. I couldn't say what I was feeling; I couldn't talk about my experiences because I believed that if I did, the Vietnamese people would surely hate me—if they knew who I was, that I had been a soldier in Vietnam. What I didn't know but found out later was that in community meetings the abbot and his assistant had told the Vietnamese residents and retreatants just who I was and why I was there, and knowing this information, the Vietnamese community seemed to love me more.

During my stay at Plum Village I was overwhelmed with feelings of guilt, and whenever I tried to talk about them with the monks and nuns, they would say, "The past is in the past. There is only the present moment and it's beautiful." One day a Mirage jet from the French air force flew at a very low level directly over the hamlets of Plum Village. The jet appeared with the unmistakable and deafening roar of a military fighter, swift and sudden, and I dove to the ground in panic. As I looked around for the carnage, the aftermath of such a swift, brutal attack, I realized that I was war reacting. I pulled myself up off the ground, shaking and in tears. The monk I was working with asked me if I was all right. I began to talk with this monk about my feelings in the moment, and he began with the "the past is in the past, there is only the present moment and it's beautiful" mantra. I responded angrily to this monk, in fact I was so angry that I almost hit him with a shovel. Instead of hitting him, I yelled: "The past is not always in the past, sometimes it's in the present moment and it's not beautiful and I hate it!" I talked about this incident with the abbot's assistant, and she explained that while it is true that the past is in the past, and there is only the present moment, if you are living intensely in the present moment, the past and the future are also here. "One just needs to learn how to live with this experience like still water." Her words, this image, helped me.

After that first visit in 1990, I returned to the monastery often. In 1992 Thich Nhat Hanh invited me to wear the robes of a monk. Having no intention of becoming a monk and feeling very uneasy with his gesture, I said to him: "I can't wear the clothes that monks wear; I'm not interested in being a Buddhist monk." He looked at me and smiled, put his hand on my shoulder, and said: "You are more of a monk than a monk." And he announced to all the people sitting there that I was a "Tao master." Everybody had a good laugh, probably because we all sensed that the abbot had just made a very profound statement; at that moment we simply could not understand the full meaning of it, and so we laughed nervously.

Although it seemed to me that this was my first contact with Buddhism, in fact I had indirectly begun the study of Zen when I was fourteen years old. At that time I studied karate, a Korean style called Hap Ki Do. At the age of sixteen I was invited to live for nine months as a monk with my teacher, and although this introduced me to Zen practice, it was a practice without the Buddha's teaching. Zen without the Buddha's teaching is dangerous.

You develop a very deep sense of concentration, tap into the power concentration without the guidance of the Buddha's transformative insights into the nature of our suffering—and the ever-present dangers of selfish desire, craving, and ignorance. I went on to study in yet another martial tradition, Chinese in origin, and by 1989 I was very involved not only in the study of these ancient arts but also in teaching them.

By the time I went to Plum Village, I had been studying and teaching karate for twenty-seven years. I had taught at five different schools and had instructed many students. There were, of course, lapses in my practice of the martial arts. There were several years after returning from Vietnam when I was lost in my suffering and trapped in my dependence on drugs and alcohol. But when I cleaned up, I returned to the martial arts, and then one day in 1989, while teaching a class of advanced students, I realized that what I was actually doing was watering the seeds of violence, that I was teaching people how to fight and to kill, and I understood that I could not continue to do this; so I stopped.

By my stopping and calming, the violence of the martial arts had the opportunity to be transformed. The robes of a martial artist became the robes of a monk. I didn't realize this transition immediately; it was only after Thich Nhat Hanh invited me to give a talk for the first time. He asked me to speak at a retreat for helping professionals being held at Plum Village. It was the very first time that I spoke publicly about Vietnam, my actions during the war, and the resulting effects. It was also the first time that I had spoken in front of a group of nonveterans.

From that first talk came the invitation to speak more, then invitations to facilitate mindfulness meditation retreats. I found that this expanded my own path of healing. It was through one of these invitations to speak that I connected with the Zen Community of New York, which led me to a meeting with its abbot, Bernie Glassman (Baisen Tetsugen Roshi). He invited me to become ordained as a novitiate in the Japanese Soto Zen Buddhist tradition, which was the beginning of my path to taking monk's vows in that tradition. So the karate ghi, the robes of fighting, were transformed through the practice of meditation— stopping and becoming calm—into the robes of peace.

Since my ordination as a Zen novitiate and subsequently as a monk, my efforts have been directed toward actualizing the image of the light at the tip of the candle. I participate in and facilitate mindfulness meditation retreats, retreats in which I live as a homeless person, and mindfulness meditation retreats in which writing has a key role (a practice I was introduced to by writer and activist Maxine Hong Kingston). I've also taken up the practice of pilgrimage. In the tradition of the ancient Zen monks of China and Japan, I take a begging bowl and only the most minimum of possessions, and I walk from one place to another. My intention is to meet whatever life puts in front of me, to experience life directly. I have walked in this way from Auschwitz, Poland, to Vietnam and from New York to California (my experiences on these pilgrimages are presented later in this book).

After taking novitiate vows, I also began to teach meditation practice to veterans and prisoners. The tools of meditation serve as a bridge for those who are interested in and committed to moving from a place of violence to a place of nonviolence. I also go into active war zones and work with soldiers, noncombatants, and refugees using the tools of meditation, of living more consciously, as a bridge from violence to nonviolence.

What I have discovered through meditation practice is that I have long wanted to work with all who are affected by violence, by the many expressions of war. Although I strongly felt this call to service, I wasn't entirely sure of how to do this. I just knew that this was somehow very important and that I had to do something. I saw that most nonveterans did not understand veterans. I knew that most nonveterans around the world do not realize their responsibility in war or how deeply they are affected by it. I also felt a deep need to bring attention to the transgenerational effects of war and the inheritance of suffering. It is important to realize that veterans are not the only ones who bear responsibility for the atrocities of war. Nonveterans sanction war, support the waging of war, supported troops being sent to Vietnam—and it is nonveterans who so often turn their backs on the returning soldiers in an effort to avoid their own complicity in the war.

When I came back from Vietnam, it was to a society and culture that attempted to wash its hands of its responsibility in that war by marginalizing those who had served. This clearly communicated that those who served were the ones who were responsible and that those who did not serve were somehow absolved of responsibility. But if we look deeply into this matter, we can know that those who don't fight are not separate from those who fight; we are all responsible for war. War is not something that happens external to us; it is an extension of us, its roots being within our very nature. It happens within all of us.

When I talk with other veterans of the Vietnam War or the Persian Gulf War, or with Russian veterans of their war in Afghanistan, Cambodian veterans of their civil war, Bosnian soldiers, Croatian soldiers, Serbian soldiers, Kosovo Liberation Army soldiers, soldiers from any war, I hear the same story. They say that they are not understood and that nonveterans avoid contact with them, resisting all but the most superficial connection. I believe that nonveterans don't make the effort to understand us because to touch the reality of our experience would mean that they would have to touch the same sort of pain and suffering inside themselves and consequently recognize their responsibility.

The fact that war puts soldiers in a position to kill people, to act violently, doesn't mean that noncombatants don't have the same potential. We can pretend that we're not violent. Whenever we are confronted with violence, we as individuals and as a society can attempt to hide from it, we can attempt to ignore it, we can attempt to push it away. But if we don't touch this part of ourselves, if we don't own our complicity in the many wars that are being fought around the world and at home, if we don't become aware of our own potential for violence, then we're not whole, we're not balanced.

What does it say about our culture that we seem to thrive on violence, both real and staged, that violence has become a media staple? When violence strikes close to home, such as at the shootings at Columbine High School, we look for an excuse—the psychopathology of the adolescents, their dysfunctional families—rather than recognizing that the actions of these young men are one reflection of the ethos of the larger society.

Everyone has their Vietnam

All veterans of violence—war violence, street violence, domestic violence—are the light at the tip of the candle and can be a powerful force for healing in the world. The way to that healing is through our suffering—looking deeply at the nature of ourselves, talking freely about how we feel, creating a language of feelings and using it to begin to break the silence that is so necessary to protect and sustain cycles of aggression.

We may think there is some safety in keeping silent, keeping the story of our trauma to ourselves, but there isn't any safety. None. If we keep these stories to ourselves, or if we keep the most important parts to ourselves, that doesn't mean that people won't know about them or that they won't affect us. It's like standing in the middle of a desert with a blanket over our heads and thinking that because we're concealing the truth of our situation, we won't die of thirst. That's insanity—and a form of self-abuse. The responsibility to begin the process of healing, to begin telling our stories, rests with each of us individually. We are the light at the tip of the candle. We have the ability to pierce the darkness of denial: our society's and our own. We have to talk. We must talk.

I have always known that the story of violence needed to be told. I knew it instinctively. But there seemed to be no way to tell it and no one interested to hear. People weren't listening because they didn't really want to know. They didn't have the willingness and in some cases the capacity to understand what I was talking about. At first, I didn't understand what I was talking about either. I just knew I needed to talk about my experience, and talk about it, and talk about it, and talk about it. It is true for all who have experienced trauma. And we have all experienced the trauma of violence in our lives directly or indirectly: an acquaintance killed by a drunk driver; a friend recounting childhood abuse; the endless scenes of war played out daily on television, in newspapers and magazines; the daily bombings, shootings, and other attacks in Israel and Palestine, Sri Lanka, Kashmir; the events at Ruby Ridge, Waco, Oklahoma City; the attacks of September 11, 2001.

An acquaintance of mine commented that *post-traumatic stress* seems too trivial a term for the profound inner wounds left by violence, for spiritual wounding that is so deep and lasting. In fact, the label *post-traumatic stress* sometimes seems just a convenient box into which we can put our experience in order to make it seem more manageable.

The physical wounds of war and violence, although significant, are less significant than the wounds that cannot be seen. The wounds of the soul, the spiritual wounds, the psychological wounds, are far deeper. You can treat physical wounds; you can manage them. People can see them and acknowledge them. The wounds of the spirit, the wounds of the soul, the wounds of the psyche—these can't be seen as clearly. For example, people say that Vietnam veterans exhibit antisocial behavior. But it's just that there is no way for us to relate in a traditional social way after our experiences in war. That was taken away from us.

But I don't want to focus just on Vietnam. Vietnam was a particular event, the Second World War was a particular event, and the Korean War was a particular event. Abuse in a family is a particular event, even if that event is repeated over and over as it so often tragically is. All of these things, all of this is war. Everyone has their Vietnam—everyone. At some level, some place, everyone has their wounds.

And everyone can become the light at the tip of the candle. We have the ability through our experience to help in the transformation of the world, to transform the violence, to transform the hate, to transform the despair.

3

The Bell of Mindfulness

Some years ago I was in Paris visiting a friend and we were traveling on the subway. It was evening, and the subway car was quite crowded. I felt something peculiar on my leg and realized that someone was attempting to put his hand into my pocket. Without thinking, I reached down, trapped the hand, and in a fluid motion pulled it up and out in preparation to break the arm at the elbow. It was an instinctive response. But at the exact moment I made this movement, I caught my breath and stopped. This happened in a split second; I didn't think about it. I held on to the hand, looked the person in the eye, and said in a loud voice: "Hey, what are you doing, putting your hand into my pocket? That's not okay! Do you need some help or something? If you need something, ask me!" The man became very apologetic and defensive, his eyes grew wide, his face blanched white, and he couldn't get out of the train fast enough. After that, two other people said that he had tried to pick their pockets as well.

Breaking the pickpocket's arm wouldn't have solved anything; it would just have created more suffering. But if this incident had happened right after I came home from

Vietnam, I doubt I would have been able to restrain myself from doing it. My first instinct would have been to act automatically from a conditioned place, a trained place, as I have done throughout much of my life. What made me stop this time? As I pulled the man's hand up and out, this act, and its accompanying thoughts, feelings, and perceptions, became like a bell ringing, a bell of mindfulness.

My encounter with Buddhism introduced me to conscious living, paying attention to the smallest detail of thought, feeling, and perception, and the term that defines this way of living is *mindfulness*. As a way of living, mindfulness helps me to wake up to and move out of cycles of destructiveness and suffering. Living mindfully, with more awareness, is not a new approach; this teaching has existed for more than twenty-six hundred years. It is not a specifically Buddhist teaching, although it was taught explicitly by the Buddha as part of the Eightfold Path.* Mindfulness expresses the heart of all spiritual teachings, and the heart of all spiritual teachings is mindfulness. Mindfulness is simply being completely in the present moment, here, now. It is recognizing that there is nothing else but this moment. Buddhism offers some powerful practices that can aid us in realizing what pulls us away, again and again, from living fully in the here and now—one of the most important of which is breath awareness.

It is so easy to get lost in the past or the future. That's what was happening to me when I was caught up in my war

---

*The Buddha described eight essential tools that when followed lead to the cessation of suffering: right view, right intention, right speech, right discipline, right livelihood, right effort, right mindfulness, and right concentration.

experiences. I was caught in the memories of the monks shooting, the booby-trapped baby, the village destroyed. I was caught in the fear that these events would happen again. I was trapped in a state of constant replay. I couldn't live in the present moment. I didn't know how to. All I could do was run from the past and hide from the future. I was trapped in the habitual pattern of either attaching or rejecting: I was attached to my conditioned understandings, how I had been taught to respond to the world and be in the world, and I rejected any information that did not agree with my concepts, my conditioning—anything that brought me in closer contact with my pain.

Breath awareness

One of the tools that I have been given to help me to be in the present moment is breath awareness. To just breathe and be aware that I am breathing. If I am completely aware of my breath, I cannot be in any other place except in the present.

You can see and experience this for yourself. Try it right now: Sit comfortably and place your hand on your abdomen. As you breathe in, feel your abdomen rise. As you breathe out, feel your abdomen contract. In . . . out . . . . Move your center of activity from your thought process to your breath. Just be present with your breath. If your mind starts to wander, allow the act of wandering to be like a soft, gentle bell ringing, inviting you back to your breath; just come back to your breath. With each conscious breath know that you are living in the present moment, that you are developing your ability to live in mindfulness.

Mindfulness, a more profound awareness, is not something that we can direct, that we can create with our thinking self. Mindfulness is a state of existence that arises as we become more aware of our habitual impulses, our conditioned nature, our patterns of thought and behavior, and begin to stop allowing these habits to dictate how we respond to the world. Mindfulness does not automatically make me feel less invaded by thoughts and memories, but rather it helps me to live in a more harmonious relationship with them. By placing my awareness on my breath, I come to see that thoughts are just thoughts—that they shift and change, coming and going like passing clouds. We can easily become so caught up in our thoughts, trapped in the illusion that they are reality. By focusing on the breath, I become the observer of my thoughts, feelings, and perceptions, neither attaching to them nor rejecting them. This is the practice of mindfulness. This is the practice that leads to liberation and peace.

There are still times when my experiences of the war are right here in the present moment. As these thoughts, feelings, and perceptions enter strongly into my consciousness, I concentrate on neither attaching to what comes up nor rejecting it. Instead I focus on just breathing, and at the same time working to establish a different relationship, a more harmonious relationship with this suffering. This does not mean that these thoughts, feelings, and perceptions go away, because they do not. Healing is not the absence of suffering. What happens is that through this process of being more present to my own life, I stop attempting to reject suffering. This is healing and transformation. Mindfulness meditation practice supports me in becoming present to the reality of my life without judgment.

To live in the present moment and find peace in our lives, we need to be mindful in all that we do, in every action that we take: the way we open the door, the way we put the dish on the shelf, the way we do our work, the way we talk to another person, the way we tie our shoes, take a step, stand up, sit down, brush our teeth, drive the car. It is not always easy. We are easily distracted by our thoughts, images of the past and the future, our dreams, our hopes, our regrets. So while living in the Vietnamese community in France, I learned the practice of using a bell to remind me to come back to my breath, a bell of mindfulness. During the abbot's talks and retreats, a bell rings from time to time. When we hear the bell, it is an invitation to come back to our breath.

The bell of mindfulness is not only a Buddhist tradition. In the Middle Ages it was a Christian tradition: When the church bell rang, it was an invitation to stop work and reflect for a moment on the gifts one had received and on the nature of one's life.

I can get so lost in the past or the future that sometimes I carry a bell with me, and I use it many times when I am giving talks to let everyone stop and breathe and simply be in the present. But it isn't necessary to carry a literal bell. If we want to, we can find bells of mindfulness everywhere. If we listen carefully, the bell of mindfulness rings constantly around us. Perhaps church bells still ring regularly in your city. The telephone can also be a bell of mindfulness. The movement and sound of a car going down the street can be a bell of mindfulness, inviting me to return to my breathing. When the traffic light turns red, it is an invitation for me to stop the hectic rush and return to my breath. When I hear a dog barking, it is an invitation to stop and breathe. My grasp on the pickpocket's hand was an invitation to stop and breathe. All these things can be bells of mindfulness for us. They bring us back to our breath in the present moment, which is all there is.

You can look deeply into your life and find many bells of mindfulness that can help bring you back to your breath. This morning I was pouring milk on my cereal and I spilled some. This was a bell of mindfulness. Last night I could not sleep, and while I was outside taking a walk, I heard sounds that seemed to me to be gunshots. For me this is a bell of mindfulness. While I was stepping outside today in a rush to get to the next place, absorbed in some thought of the next thing, a cell phone rang, bringing me back to the moment. This was a bell of mindfulness for me. Later, as I was walking, many cars passed me along the road raising clouds of dust, and naturally I thought they were going too fast. This thought was a bell of mindfulness. Rather than being drawn into the fears, thoughts, and judgments and acting from this place of suffering, I came back to my breath, becoming the observer, neither rejecting nor attaching, so that I could bear witness to how I participated in and perpetuated cycles of suffering. It is here, at this point, this exact point of the present moment —grasping the pickpocket's wrist, driving in traffic, or spilling milk—that I have the freedom of choice to act differently, to not simply react as I have in the past.

The causes and conditions of our lives trap us in suffering

I spent most of my life living in a state of forgetfulness. What a joy it is to wake up! Living in mindfulness means awakening. Sometimes when I wake up in the morning, I am consumed by suffering, full of fear, full of doubts, full of shame. But then I feel this shame as a bell of mindfulness. I breathe in and breathe out, and I am grateful to be free to touch these emotions, to establish a different relationship with them, to be able to have the possibility to make different choices in my life. When I live in forgetfulness, I have no choice. My conditioned nature is deciding for me.

The Buddhist teachings describe this forgetful state as a form of hell, the Embracing Pillar Hell. As it is described in one of the Buddhist sutras, those who fall into this hell see a pillar and take it to be a some object of desire or obsession. When they rush to embrace the pillar, it becomes red hot and sears them to death, after which they are revived (by a "clever breeze"), only to repeat the process again and again. In Buddhist tradition, hell is not just thought of as a place we might go when we die. It is also understood as a state of consciousness that we can enter at any time during our lives.

If we live in forgetfulness, we can easily fall into such a hell realm. Each of us will see the pillar differently, according to the unique circumstances of our lives. But trapped in forgetfulness, we can't resist clinging to our desires (the burning pillar) and to our conditioning (the clever breeze), and so we remain trapped in an endless cycle of suffering, repeating the dynamic again and again. In this process we even get to the point of infecting our children with our pain and lack of awareness. Unfelt suffering spreads "transgenerationally," as my own story demonstrates. And so the cycle continues from birth through death to rebirth, time and again.

We must become aware of the causes and conditions that trap us in suffering. By "causes and conditions" I mean our formative life experiences and how these experiences exhibit themselves in our actions. For me, within my experiences in childhood and in the war exist the seeds of my suffering. The many ways in which this suffering manifests itself in my actions are the causes and conditions of my life. Let me give a specific example. I don't sleep very much at night. I haven't been able to since an early experience in the war. One evening we came to a place where we parked our helicopters for the night. At some point either late in the night or early in the morning, the Vietcong overran our perimeter, the protection that surrounded us. Of the 135 or so Americans present, only 15 or 20 were not killed or wounded. I happened to be one of those few.

In the course of this night the fighting became very intense, hand-to-hand. I had to take lives with my hands. As the fighting subsided, I then had to listen to the screaming of the wounded and the dying. I had to shoot people without knowing clearly who I was shooting because everyone was everywhere. It was a most insane, chaotic, and overwhelming experience. After physically surviving this experience, I made the decision that I would not sleep at night because the night wasn't safe. The night never felt safe to me again, nor would I ever trust someone else with my safety. I made this decision consciously, not to trust anyone, because I heard later that the perimeter was breached, the position overrun, because the people who were given the responsibility to guard the perimeter fell asleep.

Even after I returned home from the war, and even now so many years later, the night can become terrible for me, or at best unsettling. As night approaches, I feel enormous anxiety because I am supposed to sleep but I can't! When the night comes, I can still hear the sounds of war, and I become hyperalert. For a long time I took drugs to make myself sleep. I took drugs because I could not accept the whole of myself, including my anxiety; I could not live in the present moment. Instead I kept trying to control the nature of things. I believed that it was me who was choosing to take drugs, drink alcohol, smoke cigarettes, rather than the seeds of suffering in my life choosing for me. I lived under the illusion of having a choice.

If I am not living in mindfulness and I have no awareness of the seeds of suffering and the causes and conditions of my life, then they control me. I can think I am making choices, but my choices are really dictated by my suffering. My unaddressed suffering leads me to act in ways I may not want to. It may have me associating with people I may not want to associate with, doing things I do not want to do, all the while telling myself that I am choosing to do those things.

As it turns out, my life was miserable as long as I resisted my inability to sleep. But there came a point, through mindfulness practice, through a willingness to live intensely in the present moment, that I simply accepted this fact: I can't sleep. At that moment of acceptance, I felt a peace I have rarely experienced before. A peace with my unpeacefulness.

One of the mistakes people often make when they take up the practice of mindfulness is that they form a false image of it. They think that being mindful means not being afraid, that it means being calm and at peace at all times. This is not living in mindfulness. Mindfulness and mental calm are related, but they are not the same. For me living in mindfulness means that I can live peacefully in nonpeace, that I can accept the reality of noncalm. In all our lives, there are moments of calm and moments of noncalm. If I live in mindfulness, I can accept that these moments come and go like a gentle tropical rain or a hurricane, but they do come and go. In mindfulness I see their beauty when they are here, I can celebrate what they offer me, knowing that they will pass and also knowing that they may return. If I am living in mindfulness, if I can look deeply into the nature of myself and touch my suffering, I can learn to live with my fear, my doubts, my insecurity, my confusion, my anger. My task is to dwell in these places like still water, as Sister Chan Khong told me during my first visit to Plum Village.

If I can continue to live mindfully, I have the opportunity of becoming like still water, but I am not there yet. There are many times when I'm touched by the anger and the violence of our society, and I react. I still have those seeds in me. But I have learned not to be so harsh with myself, because I can come back to my breath. I don't have to continue on a path I know and experience to be self-destructive.

If we do not live in mindfulness, it means we are living in forgetfulness, controlled by the causes and conditions of our life, and in this way we remain trapped in our suffering and we can be sure that we are creating more of it. It is my honest desire not to create more suffering but to awaken to the nature of the suffering so that it can become transformed.

There are a million voices, both within me and in the world, that try to distract me from my suffering. When I hear a bell of mindfulness and I come back to my breath, these voices become weaker. The bell silences them. Then my suffering can emerge. I can touch it, swim in it, and I am no longer so tempted to hide from it or to drown in it.

Healing is not the absence of suffering

A number of years ago I spent a month in Vietnam. I was on a pilgrimage that began in Auschwitz, where I had received my lay ordination in the Soto Zen tradition. Before I went, people said to me: "Why do you want to go back to Vietnam? What is the point of raking up old wounds?" And again: "The past is in the past." There was a time when I wanted to believe this. I wanted the pain to go away, to vanish without a trace as if it had never existed. I believed that healing was synonymous with the absence of pain and suffering. But through living in mindfulness, I am learning the real meaning of healing: learning how to live in relationship with my pain.

Living in mindfulness, I am invited to touch, to embrace the nature of my suffering without judging it. My emotions are neither right nor wrong, good nor bad; they simply are. Without judgment, there is much more freedom in my life. I was conditioned by my culture to judge my suffering, to feel that when I touched certain emotions I was doing something wrong. For example, when I felt rage toward noncombatants during the war and civilians after the war, I thought, "How can I feel such emotions? People tell me I should forget the past and move on." But I couldn't and didn't.

My judgment, a product of conditioned behavior, kept me trapped in forgetfulness, distant from awareness. My judgment kept me trapped in my suffering and at the same time trapped in the illusion that I was not suffering. When living in mindfulness I can be present to my inner life without judgment.

If I live in mindfulness, I have real choices, I have freedom. I will be able to hear the faint but firm voice that directs and leads me, the gentle voice of wisdom that tells me: "Claude Anshin, this is not a good idea, perhaps it is better not to do this." Or "Claude Anshin, this is a lovely idea, go for it!" The more I live in mindfulness, breathing in and breathing out, the more my life shows me the path to take. But I always have to be alert, aware, constantly vigilant. I must always look very deeply, ever deeper into the nature of my actions.

It is not possible to live in mindfulness and destroy life. When I killed in the war, I was controlled by forgetfulness. I convinced myself that they, the enemy, were the cause of my suffering. But the enemy is not the source of my suffering; my suffering is mine.

At one point after I returned from Vietnam, I was living on the street. I was homeless and lost again in forgetfulness. If you had passed near me you might have kicked me; you certainly would not have wanted to look at me. No one wants to look at this kind of desperation, because when people looked at me they saw a part of themselves they would rather believe did not exist.

It seems that in this society we are conditioned to think that we are different. Different from the homeless, the drug addicted, the murderers, the child molesters, but we are not different. We may not be any of these things, but this does not mean that we are different. If we live without awareness, without looking deeply at ourselves, we too can find ourselves homeless, in prison, divorced, a rapist, or a molester. Unaddressed suffering can take us to these places so quickly that we have no idea how we got there or often even that we are there. And what is more troubling is that in the midst of being controlled by our unacknowledged pain, trapped in our suffering, we think that we are not. We think that we are aware. This is the power of illusion, the taproot of forgetfulness.

But in reality, there is no separation between ourselves and others. Mindfulness takes us beyond the idea of "me" as separate and gives us the clarity to see the point at which we are not separate from that which we perceive as other. We are not different. I am not you and we are not different. The next time you meet a homeless person on the street, look at her, touch him, let them be a bell of mindfulness for you, and know that you are not different. When we recognize that we are no different, then we do not need to look away with guilt and shame. We can see the humanity and the suffering and choose whether to help or not from a place of compassion and acceptance rather than judgment and denial.

The moment will come when we are not controlled by our desperation

If we live in mindfulness, the moment will come when we are not controlled by our desperation, when we are no longer driven by the seductions of our suffering because all experience becomes an act of meditation. Life becomes clearer, more fluid, more simple—though not necessarily easier. As the Buddha taught, life is suffering. This does not go away when we practice mindfulness—but what we think, feel, and do in the face of this suffering will change.

Every act in life can become an act of meditation and a pathway to compassion. To drink water, to speak with a friend, to look at a tree, to listen to the trucks passing by, to blow your nose, to cough, to go to the toilet—everything.

If I live mindfully, I do not have to stop to meditate. However, to reinforce the reality of mindfulness in my life, it is also important to find a quiet place each day where I can sit still on a cushion, chair, rock, whatever. It can be any place—in my room, in a train, on a plane, sitting in a park. Creating this space for myself is very important. This moment of quiet allows me to listen to the interior voice that guides me. (Instructions for beginning your own sitting meditation practice are offered in the appendix.) The more I am able to live in mindfulness, the more that voice can speak to me in any moment. It is not like someone talking to me inside my head; it is a feeling of the correctness of my action or perhaps only an invitation to stand still.

In my experience of meditation, as I bring my awareness back to my breath, becoming calm and still, the things that I turn my attention to right themselves. For example, if I am distracted while I am sitting in meditation, my body may adopt an awkward position. When the bell of mindfulness rings and I suddenly realize what is happening, I return to the present moment and return my body to a more supportive position. Or if I am lost in my thoughts, I realize this and become mindful of my mind. The thoughts become calmer and pass like the clouds in the sky.

We do not need to be sitting in a meditation hall to breathe and to practice meditation. We could sit on a cushion until we are ninety, but if we are not deeply mindful of our breath, we are not practicing meditation. Mindfulness does not mean studying Buddhism or certain forms of meditation. It is the way we are, the way we live. If we live in mindfulness, every action of our life becomes meditative.

So I invite you to practice mindful living. Be aware that you are breathing, be aware of your thinking self, be aware of your feeling self, and be aware of your sense self—your smell, taste, sight, hearing, touch, even the touch of the clothes on your skin at this moment. Be deeply aware of this, the nature of yourself and of all that is happening around you. Touch this—experience it in the present moment. This is the nature of life, the nature of your life.

At each bell of mindfulness—whether it's a traffic light, a telephone ring, or a homeless person—breathe in and breathe out, inviting the present moment fully, for it is wonderful in all that it brings us.

I would rather not have killed, but I have killed. And to reject that is to reject myself and the reality of my actions. Through mindfulness practice, living in the present moment, I'm able to invite my whole self into my life, to integrate all the different parts of myself into one whole. Yes, I am the little boy playing baseball and I am the soldier killing. Yes, I am the drug addict using heroin, and I am the father of a wonderful boy. I am all of these things, and I must not turn away from any of them. As I welcome all of these elements of myself into the present moment, I am able to participate more fully in my life.

We are all like stones, you know. If someone takes us and throws us in a pond, the ripples will fill the pond. If we live in forgetfulness, nonmindfulness, our suffering will fill the pond. But if we live in mindfulness, our healing will fill the pond.

4

If You Blow Up a Bridge, Build a Bridge

During the time that I was in Vietnam, I was responsible for a tremendous amount of death and destruction. At the retreat where I first heard Thich Nhat Hanh speak, I wanted to apologize through him to the Vietnamese people, to make amends to them in some way for all that killing. But I didn't know how to begin. When I finally worked up the nerve to ask someone, I approached his assistant, Sister Chan Khong, with the question: "How do I atone for the destruction that I was responsible for in Vietnam?" She said to me: "If you blow up a house, then you build a house. If you blow up a bridge, then you build a bridge." I asked her, "But if I kill a person, how do I make that right?" Her answer was that I was not responsible for my actions—but I knew that I had asked her a question that she couldn't really answer. It was here, at this point, that I had to find my own way.

As a soldier I had been trained to kill; that is the point of military training, after all. I had been conditioned to believe that the path to peace passed through killing. I was taught that everything that was different from me, that threatened my beliefs, was my enemy; that the only objective in life was victory; and that victory was accomplished through the defeat and destruction of the enemy.

As I've explained, I was trained to cut myself off from my emotions, to repress them. This created a separation from the essential life force that is our humanity and enabled me to kill. Ultimately I was taught a certain way of looking at myself: I learned to see myself as a separate self, not connected with anything, and the ruler over all things.

Yet all the spiritual traditions—Buddhist, Christian, Muslim, Jewish, and all the others I know of—tell us that all life is connected, interdependent, and sacred. The Buddha's teachings emphasize our profound interconnectedness. That, in fact, I'm not different from the piece of paper on which I'm writing. And while it's true that I'm no different from this piece of paper, it's also true without any doubt that I'm not this piece of paper. Now you might be thinking, "What is all this gibberish? Is this guy nuts?" Let me explain myself.

Within this piece of paper there are what we can identify as many nonpaper elements. As we all know, paper comes from trees. But where do trees come from? They come from the earth and rely on the sun and the rain. When we consider this, we can see that in this sheet of paper the earth is here, the sky is here, the rain is here, the minerals from the soil are here, the wind is here. Lovingkindness is also here, expressed as the gift that this paper gives us by carrying these words. All of those same nonpaper elements also exist within me. The human body is 60 to 70 percent water; all the trace elements and many of the minerals that one finds in the earth can also be found in our body and are essential to maintaining a healthy existence. The sky exists in us as the air that we breathe that sustains our life.

So there isn't any real separation between the universe and me. The universe is within me. The whole universe exists right here in this very moment. I talk from the perspective of Buddhist practice because that is where my focus is just now, but the essence of all spiritual practice, regardless of its name, is to bring us to an awareness of the intrinsic interconnectedness of all that is. Everything that I do affects the world around me. My actions, in fact, affect the whole universe. If I abuse or mistreat this piece of paper, I am abusing or mistreating myself, abusing or mistreating you.

The first Buddhist precept is not to kill. Aware of the suffering caused by the destruction of life, I vow not to kill, not to let others kill, not to condone any act of killing in my life. Keeping this precept helps me wake up to all the ways in which I might precipitate acts of killing. When I drink a glass of water, I realize that I am killing. "How is this?" you might ask. Well, there are microorganisms in this water. So when I drink it I'm killing those microorganisms. Now you might say, "Oh, they're only microorganisms, no big deal. How can you compare a microorganism to human life?" I've heard that argument quite often. My response is that the moment I see myself as separate from those microorganisms, I start creating a hierarchy, and then doing what I did in Vietnam becomes plausible. It's only a few short steps away.

But I have to drink the water to stay alive, so what do I do? The practice for me then is to accept that I am not separate from the water, not separate from the microorganisms, and as I drink the water, I do so with the conscious awareness of the ramifications of this action and so I drink each sip of water with the reverence it deserves. I turn the drinking of water into an act of spiritual practice, an act of consciousness awareness, because it is also true that if I don't drink the water, then I am also killing, because I would die without water.

A while ago I read the book *On Killing* by Dave Grossman, a lieutenant colonel who taught at one of the military colleges. In this book he explores the psychology of killing and writes that if the military took away the guns and the planes and the bombs, there would be less killing because you would have to come in close, be involved directly in the act, and most people don't want to do that. It's easier to believe you are not responsible if you don't have to see or touch the other person. However, the fact is that even at a distance we are still responsible. I am still responsible.

In the ten-year period declared by the U.S. government to be the Vietnam War, approximately 58,000 American soldiers were killed. In this country, from 1991 to 1999, gun violence killed 29,000 to 39,500 people *annually*.* Conservatively then, more than 260,000 people were violently killed in this country during a nine-year period—more than four times the number of Americans killed in Vietnam. By any other name, this is still a war. Yes, that's right, there is a serious war being fought right here on U.S. soil. And I must look to see the point at

---

*Tom W. Smith, "2001 National Gun Policy Survey of the National Opinion Research Center: Research Findings" (research study, University of Chicago, 2001).

which I am responsible. I'm responsible for every one of those handgun deaths. You may wonder how I can believe that I am responsible. If I don't speak up, if I don't make an active choice to live differently, if I live in ignorance, then I am not absolved from responsibility for all the manifestations of violence in the world. With my intimate understanding and experience of violence, it is my responsibility to bring more and more awareness to these conditions. This is my spiritual work.

What I have come to understand is that I can't directly stop any of the many wars that are being fought around the world, including the domestic war fought with handguns. But if I can wake up to the fact that I am responsible, and if I can wake up to the war inside me, then I can bring an end to fighting by healing my war. This happens as I wake up to the nature of my suffering, the causes and conditions of my life, and begin doing things differently.

If I realize the teaching of interconnectedness, then I can come to a place of understanding, a place beyond the intellect. A place where I am not separate from anything. And here I will discover that I have an impact, that my actions have an impact on the whole world.

While living and studying in Plum Village, the Buddhist monastery in France, I kept asking myself a question over and over. It was the question of cause and effect (or karma), turning negative causal relations into positive ones. It was the question of atonement. What could I do about the lives that I had taken? I can't reconstruct them. What I am discovering through Buddhist practice, however, is that by waking up, by not perpetuating suffering but living consciously and differently, I can begin to repair what I have done. I've come to believe that the universe does not work by simple negative or positive arithmetic: an eye for an eye, a tooth for a tooth; a bridge for a bridge. By decreasing the reservoir of pain and suffering, we can save lives and even create new life.

I have to do things differently. But I cannot think myself into a new way of living, I have to live myself into a new way of thinking. For me, the answer lies in trying to live a life of service and do what reveals itself as positive and useful. The direction that this service has taken is helping others, because I wouldn't be here if people hadn't helped me. So atonement, for me, means making a commitment to living in conscious awareness and offering to others what I have learned from Buddhism about healing the wars inside us. This is the path that I have taken to help decrease the violence in the world. Violence that I have been directly responsible for.

Becoming a monk

As mentioned earlier, during one of my visits to the monastery in France (where I lived and studied for the better part of three years), I was invited to become ordained as a monk in the tradition practiced there. I declined because I didn't want to live a cloistered, monastic life. Sadly, when I made this decision, Thich Nhat Hanh's connection and commitment to me changed significantly. The support I had been receiving was suddenly withdrawn. So I left Plum Village and returned to the States.

In the States I was introduced to Bernie Glassman, an American Soto Zen teacher. Following our initial meeting I called him and said I would like to meet with him in private to talk about the work he was doing with an international community of social activists engaged in peacemaking and Zen practice.

About two or three weeks later I went to Yonkers, New York, where he lived. We sat together in meditation for about fifteen minutes. When we finished sitting, he opened the conversation by saying, "I would like to ordain you."

Although at a deep level I wanted to take this step, my response was, "Why do you want to ordain me? What's your motive? I mean, you don't even know me!" When I raised my concerns, he said, "I know you enough."

Accepting Bernie's invitation did not mean that I would live apart from the world in a monastery. So I finally said, "Yes, I'm interested. What's next?"

There would be several ordinations, and they took place in phases: First I underwent a lay ordination (*jukai* in Japanese). In this ceremony I vowed to follow the sixteen observances, which include:

The Three Pure Precepts: Do no evil, do good, and do
     good for others.
The Three Treasures: A vow to be one with the Bud-
     dha, the Dharma, and the Sangha (the community).
The Ten Grave Precepts: Nonkilling, nonstealing,* not
     being greedy, not telling lies, not being ignorant,
     not talking about others' errors and faults, not ele-
     vating oneself by blaming others, not being stingy,
     not being angry, and not speaking ill of the Three
     Treasures.

---

*These terms are used instead of "not killing" and "not stealing" to indicate that abstaining from these activities is to be taken up as a spiritual practice, not simply as a prohibition or a rule.

I then went on to be ordained as a novice monk (*tokodo*). During this ceremony I received the robes of a Zen monk and my begging bowls (which are also used in the zendo, or meditation hall, during formal eating ceremonies), and my head was shaved. Later I would be ordained as a Dharma Holder (a monk who is empowered to teach), then as a senior monk (*denkai*), which gave me the authority to ordain others through all the empowerments up to Denkai. I have also been initiated as a lifetime member of the Zen Peacemaker Order.

At the time I first agreed to being ordained, I was planning to participate in a peace pilgrimage through Eastern Europe and Asia, beginning at the site of the concentration camp at Auschwitz and traveling, mostly on foot, to Vietnam. The pilgrimage would take us through Poland, Austria, Croatia, Hungary, Serbia, Romania, Bulgaria, Greece, the West Bank, Gaza, Israel, Jordan, Iraq, India, Malaysia, Thailand, Cambodia, and for me it ended in Vietnam (others continued on to Hiroshima, Japan). I undertook this pilgrimage in the style of the wandering mendicant monks of Asia, traveling with just a few simple possessions. My goal was to bear witness to major sites of war and violence, to face them openly with mindfulness, and to talk with the people I met along the way about my experiences in war.

There were points during this pilgrimage in which we were unable to walk because of closed borders or unwillingness of governments to give us permission. In most of these instances I begged for money to purchase tickets to cover the basic cost of travel by ferry, bus, train, plane, or private car. The whole experience took eight months.

Despite my initial intentions, my experience of pilgrimage ended up being very personal. The practice of pilgrimage brought me again and again directly into contact with the war in me, my own suffering. With the tools of spiritual practice (the monastic disciplines I have received), I found that I had a foundation that supported my living differently with these realities. My vows had given me a kind of container to help me hold the intensity of my experiences.

Bernie Glassman came to Auschwitz, and my lay ordination took place there, at the site of one of the crematoriums. This was in late November and early December 1994. From there I began my journey to Vietnam. In the original plan Bernie was to come to Vietnam and ordain me as a novice monk there. As circumstances turned out, he wasn't able to do it, as his teacher, Taizan Maezumi Roshi, died in April of that year (1995), and he had to tend to all of the affairs connected with his death. So I finished the pilgrimage, returned to the States, and was ordained as a monk in Yonkers on August 6, 1995. Hiroshima Day.

Through the process of ordination I found that I had been provided with more grounding and credibility. Living as a monk gave me a kind of visual credibility. I became a symbol of the teaching that works through me. Ordination made a big difference to me because I saw accepting this step as a tremendous commitment to really live in a more conscious and responsible way.

Part of the ordination process is to get your head shaved. Initially this seemed like a stumbling block. Not only did I love my long blond hair but I associated having my head shaved with being humiliated. I decided, in spite of my resistance, to continue down the path toward ordination, keeping foremost in my mind that I could say no at any point. But I didn't, and what I discovered is that shaving

my head wasn't a sacrifice, nor was it humiliating. My ordination stood as a commitment, a very serious commitment to living in a new way.

I decided to become a monk to celebrate life, not to hide
from it. So I chose not to live in a monastery but to live more
consciously and visibly in the world. I chose to live as a wandering mendicant monk. I have taken vows not to work in
the conventional sense, not to accumulate material possessions, and to wander. As a result, I spend 260 to 265 days
per year traveling throughout the world, living a period of
each year on pilgrimage, studying, accepting invitations to
teach meditation, and also living homeless on the street.
When teaching I do not accept any compensation other
than food, shelter, and transportation. While I do return for
a period of time each year to a Zen center in the United
States, I don't own this center or live there permanently (it's
owned by a foundation that has been formed to support the
work that develops as a result of my wanderings).

In my travels I am in contact with many different spiritual communities, inviting them to meet together, because
all spiritual traditions tell us that we are not different, that
we are interconnected, and that together we are powerful.
Power is not arms to conquer; power is arms to hold and
comfort and work together for peace.

I also invite lay and monastic communities to meet together. Just because I am a monk does not mean that I am
different from you. It only means that I have chosen another path. We can learn a lot from each other. We do not
all have to do the same thing to be a powerful and harmonious community. What is necessary is that we live our
own lives committed to mindfulness.

One of the ways through which I am attempting to honor my commitment is by talking to others who are suffering from the experience of war—no matter what form their war takes, whether they are in the Balkans or living on the streets or caught in a war in their own homes. I want to help them to become aware of the reality of interconnectedness.

His enemies saved his arm, saved his life

In November of 1993 (before I was ordained) I was invited to go to the Balkans with a group of people who called themselves peace workers. One of the first places we visited was the city of Mostar, which was under siege. Mostar is divided by a river and surrounded by mountains. People on the west side of the city were firing at people on the east side, people in the east were shooting at people in the west, and people in the mountains were firing down on both sides. Each street that ran perpendicular to the river was a shooting gallery, and each side was shelling the other with mortars every day, all day long. Each side also had snipers that were randomly killing people. Every time you crossed a street, you were a target.

When I first arrived in Mostar, I noticed that people walked around as if they were on the streets of Grove City, Kansas, seemingly oblivious to the reality of war that was all around them. When I saw this I began to cry, because I knew this detached state intimately. And I knew the long-term implications of this detachment.

In Mostar (and later in Sarajevo), in hospitals and on both sides of the front, I talked with soldiers about war, about fighting and not fighting. The peace workers I was traveling with came from several different countries and sincerely wanted to promote peace. But these activists didn't ask the people of Mostar: "What can we do to help?" They had come with their own agendas, their own ideas of what peace should be, and they tried to impose them on the situation. This is not peace work but, rather, peace imperialism. In my experience this is another form of war. I realized that the activists really wanted peace; they were dedicating their lives to it. But they had no idea what peace was, only their own theoretical concepts, and they didn't have any tools to help them learn. They did not know how to breathe. No one had ever invited them to look at their own suffering, and therefore their peace activism became an extension of their suffering.

For me it was important to speak simply and authentically with people in this war zone and to realize there is nothing I can do to stop this war or any other. I can only stop the war that is within me and help others to look inside themselves.

One day we reached a hospital situated on the west side of Mostar, and the pacifist group found an injured soldier who spoke English. After an initial frenzy of microphones and video cameras, I was finally left alone with him. I invited him to talk to me about the nature of his experience in this war. In the beginning he responded to me with a kind of protective propaganda, talking only about how terrible the other side was. So I invited him to talk more openly and personally by telling him about my own experience in the Vietnam War. I talked to him about the stress of war, the sleeplessness; I talked to him about what encouraged me to go and the abandonment that I experienced when I returned. I spoke to him about the killing, about the senselessness that grew in me during my time in Vietnam and the emotional numbness that set in to cover my feelings.

I came back the next day to see him. When I walked over to his bed and our eyes met, he broke into a large smile. He was surprised that I had come back. Tears began forming in his eyes, but when he realized he was showing his emotions, he froze.

On that day we spoke about his injuries. He had been shot in the left elbow, and I asked him how it had happened. While being held as a prisoner of the east side he had been forced to dig trenches. While he was working, he had been wounded by someone shooting from the west side, a sniper from his own group. When the doctors arrived, they told him he would have to have his arm amputated at the elbow. I asked the soldier how he came to be in this hospital on the west side with his arm mostly intact. It turns out that the doctors from the east side, realizing that they could not provide him with adequate care, arranged to have him sent back to the west side. The doctors on the east side—his enemies—saved his arm, saved his life.

We talked some more about the war in the Balkans. Whenever he started to talk about the "beasts and demons" of the opposing side, I touched his arm and asked him: "What do you say about this arm?" And after a while he said: "Yes, maybe they are not all beasts. They did save me, they did save my arm."

The next day he began to speak to me about the nature of fighting and of war. I asked him: "How do you explain this war? Everywhere I go, all the people that I'm talking with are telling me they don't want it." He replied, "This is not our war, it is our grandfathers' war; they should take up arms and fight." He went on, "This is the politicians' war; it ought to be them on the front line." I came to this same feeling while serving as a soldier in the Vietnam War—it wasn't my war.

Later the soldier asked me how I had been treated by the Americans once I returned home. I replied, "They rejected me. They did not want me around because I reminded them of their responsibility for the war in Vietnam." He said, "It's no different here. When you are in the front line, everyone loves you, they give you a house, food, money . . . but when you are no longer fit to fight, they don't want you anymore."

I asked him, "Why do you fight?" He said, "If I don't fight, the beast on the other side will certainly kill us. They will overwhelm us; they will kill everybody." And then I asked him, "Why did those doctors save your arm?" He just looked at me, and I knew together we had peeled away some of the lies that sow the seeds of war.

The victor and the vanquished carry the same scars

When I left the Balkans in December, I drove to Hamburg to visit a friend and stayed there through the holiday season. The war in the Balkans was very fresh in me, and I was again wound combat tight. I was hypervigilant, ill at ease, distrusting, unable to concentrate, bombarded by intrusive thoughts. In Hamburg, Christmas and New Year's are celebrated with a lot of firecrackers. Each time a firecracker went off, I heard snipers' bullets.

One night while I was walking off my restlessness, I was looking at the buildings of Hamburg, and I began to see them as they must have looked at the end of the Second

World War, bombed and desolate, like the destroyed buildings of the Balkans. In this moment I touched what I can only imagine was the experience of the Second World War in Europe, in Germany. I heard the planes coming, the bombs falling, the buildings exploding, the children crying, the people dying, the air raid sirens and the sirens of the fire engines. I could smell it, I could feel it, I could taste it, and I sat down on a curb between two parked cars and began to cry.

All my life, at both a conscious and an unconscious level, the German people had been my enemy, and as they were the enemy, I could not touch or acknowledge the Germans as human beings. I could not come in contact with or acknowledge that they too suffered, and suffered immensely. But in that moment I could feel the suffering of the war in Germany. And in that moment I felt connected to the humanity of the German people, and more connected to my own humanity. In that moment I was not separate any longer, and they were no longer my enemy.

Whether you're the victor or the vanquished, you carry the same scars. I've been back to Vietnam, and I've listened to the suffering of the Vietcong and others who fought for North Vietnam. I spoke with wounded Vietnamese veterans at a hospital there. Just like American veterans of the war, they haven't been able to hold jobs, they haven't been able to maintain relationships, they have high rates of chemical dependence and suicide.

In Thailand I talked with a Buddhist monk in his fifties or sixties. He had fought in Laos during the Vietnam War. We talked about his experience and the experience of his friends who had served in the military. The stories that he told were not so different from mine. War and violence affect everyone in very similar ways, whether it's in Vietnam or in Thailand or in the United States.

Veterans of the Persian Gulf War were celebrated and embraced, there were parades for them. Yet, when it turned out that many were suffering from a malady that came to be known as Gulf War syndrome, this country and the agencies designated to care for these veterans once again turned their backs. The government said, "Well, we don't know; there's nothing really wrong here." Again: the societal denial of a problem, denial of our collective responsibility for the consequences of war. Veterans of all wars suffer as a result of this denial.

Is war ever justified?

I hold the position that violence is never a solution. I have been led to this view by my own experience, by our collective history, and by the truth of cause and effect. Every action brings an equal and opposite reaction—a fundamental law of physics. Though we cannot predict with certainty when the reaction will take place, how it will manifest, or to what degree, we know—and I know this very personally—that violence leads to more violence. A look at history confirms this: We see an endless succession of wars and violence, all instigated, whatever the details, with the justification that the action of war is a necessary tool to bring an end to conflict and further violence. But it never has.

At speaking and teaching engagements, when I make the pronouncement that violence is never a solution, I am often asked what I refer to as the Hitler questions. These include: "If by killing one person you could save one hundred lives, wouldn't you kill that person?" Or "If someone broke into your home and was intent on killing everyone in your family, wouldn't you use force to stop them?" Or "If there hadn't been an aggressive action mounted against Hitler, what would have been the consequences?"

These questions are of course legitimate. And they are also inherently rhetorical. I don't know what I would do if I were confronted with the kinds of situations that are often posed to me. The Second World War appears to have been successful, but is the world a safer place? Have those who aspire to gain power through the use of violence and aggression been deterred? Without a doubt the answer is no. While it is true that the violent intervention of the Second World War stopped a holocaust that had to be stopped, for me there still exists the nagging question, Did this bring an end to holocausts or to genocide?

Many people continue to believe that in certain circumstances we should kill to prevent further killing. My hope is to help people to discover what a terribly dangerous argument this is. This very argument has been used to justify preemptive strikes, to maintain a nuclear arsenal that could destroy the planet a hundred times over, to uphold the death penalty. It is being used as a rationale for the current occupations of Iraq and Afghanistan—and it was also the argument that the Fascists and the Nazis used to justify their agenda in Europe. As we can clearly see, this argument can be used to justify almost anything.

I know, unwaveringly, that violence is never the solution to humanity's problems and that the real solution resides in the ethic and value of nonviolence. Nonviolence is not, however, to be confused with being passive or complacent. Passivity, like its opposite, aggression, is a behavior of those controlled and dominated by fear. I also know that the commitment to nonviolence requires an almost complete overhaul of our conditioned nature. It requires us to live differently and demands great courage and great sacrifice.

Ultimately, all responsibility and all action begin with the individual, and so it is here that we must start. In its simplest form, nonviolence is rooted in the knowledge that we have the capacity to act violently and aggressively and that we make a conscious choice not to. Nonviolence is not succumbing to our conditioning, not succumbing to our sense of helplessness that has us deciding again and again, either actively or passively, to support the use of violence as an effective form of conflict resolution. Nonviolence means strongly standing up for truth and compassion in the midst of confrontation—and doing so without aggression.

As a soldier trained and seasoned in the savagery of war, it is my concerted effort when talking and writing about war and violence to be direct and succinct. Contrary to the pessimistic or fatalistic opinions held by many that war is inevitable, given the grim nature of the human being, it is my firm conviction and clear understanding that while conflict is inevitable, the degeneration of conflict into slaughter, mayhem, and the abject abandonment of truth is not.

We do not need war to stave off our boredom or give us meaning and definition as a people. It is not our human nature but rather our unhealed, unaddressed suffering that propels us to industrialized killing. Killing at this level is quite simply the consequence of a fear-based philosophy that drives us to seek safety by attempting the impossible: to control everything and everyone around us.

War, as so accurately described in Chris Hedges's book *War Is a Force That Gives Us Meaning*, is both myth and narcotic, one created to sell the other. From my experience I can attest to this. And the nature of addiction is that it leads us to lie and attempt to manipulate everyone and everything around us. We repeat these lies so often that we begin to believe them as truth. Healing and transformation from this deadly and ever-tightening spiral is possible. If we don't believe this, then we seal away any possibility to live differently, to live in dignity with respect and compassion for ourselves and others.

It is my intention to pass along the information that we can live differently, that war and suffering can be transformed—and not through the cataclysm that is preached by the pessimists. This awakening that I am referring to has been achieved by many before us, but not without sacrifice. It is up to those who have begun to awaken and those of us who have experienced healing and transformation to stand up, to demonstrate through the fabric of our lives that there is a solution.

What happened to me in Vietnam is not unique. Other people from many different wars can identify with what I'm talking about—even people who have never fought in a war but are veterans of violent homes and violent cultures like ours. Even though the details, the particular events, may be entirely different, there is something in my story that resonates with many people. This offers an opening for us all to begin to talk.

So when I talk, I am telling my story and also the collective story. I'm telling the story of hundreds of generations—of millions of people affected by war and violence. What is important about the telling is not so much the details of the story as the telling itself. Whenever I tell my story, it not only forces me to realize what has happened to me; it also brings me more in tune with the reality of interdependence and interconnectedness, with what Thich Nhat Hanh calls "interbeing." I see that certain events happened to me, that these events have had a clear impact on my psychological and physical existence. They shaped it. And because of these effects I am not living my life freely. I am living it as dictated by my suffering. So if I want to have some choice and freedom in my life, I need to wake up to the reality of these experiences, how they affect my life, how I act them out or how they become acted out through my person—and then acknowledge my responsibility in all of this. I find that as I begin to become more awake to the reality of my own life, I stop blaming others.

I can feel very alone in this journey because it is in fact a journey that only I can take, but I don't have to take this journey in isolation. Telling our stories, sharing them, can lead to the creation of community, a loving community committed to really living life differently. This community of like-minded people (*sangha* in the language of Buddhism) can then assist, help, support, and encourage each other in this process of waking up. This connection can and will manifest itself in many different ways. Sometimes we help each other through sitting together; sometimes by touching and holding, nurturing; sometimes through talking. We can also support each other through serving as an example, and we can help our community by taking principled actions for peace.

When we establish connection through gathering together and talking about our experience, we don't tell just the good stories. Instead, we tell the truth, talking about how we are feeling, about what we're experiencing. As we enter into this process, it is important to abandon any notion that we need to "handle" or "control" our suffering. Suffering is to be experienced and shared with others. Together we are much stronger than we are alone.

Let us be a community, a sangha. Let us support each other, with our sadness, with our loss, with our despair. Share it with others. As two can carry it better than one, just imagine how a roomful can carry it. We are all connected one to another. I am not different from you: As you suffer, I suffer; as you heal, I heal. This is how we can rebuild bridges, rebuild homes, rebuild lives. It is through this process that we can begin to experience joy, the result of waking up and learning to live harmoniously with the whole self.

The author at age 4.

Army induction photo, age 17.

In Vietnam, age 18.

In walking meditation with Thich Nhat Hanh in 1992.

With a refugee child in Croatia during the war in the Balkans, 1994.

Aboard an abandoned attack helicopter in Pleiku, Vietnam, in 1995.

At a Jewish settlement in the West Bank, 1995, during the Pilgrimage for Peace and Life (holding the base of a Buddhist prayer flag).

With Palestinian soldiers at a refugee camp during the Pilgrimage for Peace and Life.

On the American Zen Pilgrimage, bowing to a traveling replica of the Vietnam Veterans Memorial. Hamzha looks on.

Being questioned and directed by police while walking through Kansas.

Walking through Utah, on the American Zen pilgrimage.

During a street retreat (living homeless as a spiritual practice) in New York City in 1994.

5

Walking to Walk

In December 1994 I began a five-thousand-mile pilgrimage from Auschwitz, in Poland, to Vietnam. In our group there were at times as few as twenty-six of us and, crossing into Cambodia, as many as one thousand. We walked through twenty-one countries, and everyplace we walked, we passed through areas of past suffering or current suffering, past wars or current wars.

I undertook the walk initially because I was intrigued by the practice of pilgrimage, and because I had an instinctive sense that this was the way that I needed to return to Vietnam. I also wanted to see more, to check my understandings, to get in touch with the conditions of the wider human community. While walking I discovered that pilgrimage also supported me in getting in touch with my own suffering. Ultimately I went on this walk to bear witness, which is one of the core tenets of the Zen Peacemaker Order, of which I am a lifetime member.

The Zen Peacemaker Order is an effort initiated by Bernie Glassman and others to establish a loosely connected network of Zen practitioners who are socially engaged. Members of the order support each other and share ideas, techniques, and contacts in an effort to bring the world of social action into a more interconnected relationship. But as this is a relatively new initiative, its configurations and understanding of itself continue to evolve.

This pilgrimage (called the Pilgrimage for Peace and Life) was my first, but since then I have traveled frequently to areas where there is fighting. I also regularly spend time on the streets living homeless, in contact with the conditions of the disenfranchised, the marginalized, with people who are obviously suffering. Spending time on the streets with the homeless brings me again and again to the essential point at which I begin to see more clearly the roots of suffering, the roots of violence, the roots of war, and it enables me to realize the absolute necessity of shining the light of attention on our suffering.

In 1995, when I was ordained as a monk by Bernie Glassman, I took the vows of a mendicant. A mendicant is someone who does not own property, does not live in a monastery or reside with any permanence indoors, and is not gainfully employed. It's a commitment to wander as a spiritual practice.

I made the decision to take the vows of a mendicant monk primarily because I wanted to live more directly as the Buddha had (to the extent possible). Also, in witnessing the evolution of Zen Buddhist orders in the United States, I wanted to evoke the more ancient traditions of those who embarked on this spiritual path and to live my commitment more visibly.

It's also worth pointing out that my decision to live as a wandering mendicant monk was not such a great leap for me. This way of life is not very different from the marginalized existence I found myself living after my return from

Vietnam. After the war I had great difficulty getting hired or holding on to a job. I wandered from place to place (much of the time penniless), unable to sustain relationships, and so forth. I don't want to suggest here that I had already been living as a Zen Buddhist monk. Far from it. My life after the war was a desperate one lived not in an understanding of our interconnectedness but, to a large extent, in unwanted isolation. Yet, as it turned out, becoming a mendicant monk was not such a radical change in lifestyle for me.

I am, of course, living as a mendicant monk in the context of the twenty-first century, a time rooted in consumerism—in the philosophy that more is better. I am constantly witness to the devastating effects that result from this kind of grasping. Living as a mendicant, I hope to demonstrate the truth of the Buddhist teaching that material possessions are not the real source of happiness, peace, and fulfillment.

At the same time, I've come to realize that it is very important for me, through this commitment, not to grasp on to my monastic vows in a dogmatic or rigid manner. To do so would not allow me to see how these vows support me in my efforts to live a more engaged life.

Pilgrimage is commonly understood as a journey to a holy place, and a pilgrim is thought of as someone who takes such a journey as an act of devotion. This definition of pilgrimage is external: The holy place is outside; the devotion is something that I have to go someplace else to do. Through my study of Buddhism, I have come to understand pilgrimage as the journey to know one's self completely. The holy place is the self, not a place somewhere out there. Over time, I've come to understand that the holy place is a greater level of awareness developed through the journey. The practice of pilgrimage is not really about going somewhere at all. It's about opening ourselves to whatever we encounter along the way, to whatever assists or encourages us to know our selves more deeply and more intimately.

I spent the first four days of the Pilgrimage for Peace and Life fasting and chanting within the Birkenau concentration camp (Birkenau was part of the vast complex of labor and death camps at Auschwitz) at the site where the Jews and other prisoners were off-loaded from the railroad cattle cars that had transported them from different locations throughout Europe. It was here that the selection was made as to who would be sent directly to the gas chambers and who would be sent into forced labor, with the intention that they would also eventually be killed. I sat at this site and chanted a line from the Lotus Sutra (a core Buddhist scripture) with the intention of bringing great healing and awareness to this place, to these acts, and to the conditions that led to these acts. One of the things I understood while I was at Birkenau—looking at the gates of the camp, the barracks, the barbed wire, the guard towers—is that even today, at any moment, the Holocaust can repeat itself, because it does not belong to the past; it exists now. Each of us, under certain circumstances, could act with this kind of horrendous cruelty. I know this personally to be true. I must touch and accept this reality, and I must not act from the part of myself that makes holocaust possible.

During those days while I chanted and fasted, I became acutely aware not only of the suffering of the prisoners of the camps but of the suffering of all the soldiers who had been guards at Birkenau and other camps during the war. I realized that I must look at their suffering and not only at that of the prisoners. I must see the guard that is within me. If I see myself as different from the guard, there will be another Birkenau. But it will also happen if I see myself as different from the Jews or the others who were imprisoned and killed in Birkenau—communists, trade unionists, homosexuals, political dissidents, anyone perceived as a threat to the National Socialist (Nazi) state.

An important moment for me was seeing the execution wall at Auschwitz. I walked up to this wall and faced it, and then I turned my back to it. I spent some time standing there, seeing myself as one of those who faced execution. Then I walked forward, turned, and stood where the executioners stood, to see myself as one of them. Because in reality I am both. In war there is no separation. It is true that the Nazis and the Jews were different, but I must also see how they are not different, how each of us has the potential to become both the persecutor and the victim.

One day I was walking by myself along the river at Auschwitz and I sat and asked myself what it must have meant to be Polish and to live in that town during the war, aware of what was going on inside the camp; to have breakfast every morning, go to work, come back home and have dinner, to live with these conditions as normal. It must have been terrible to live in such a state of denial and numbness. For me it still is, as this sort of numbness to exploitation, abuse, and violence continues in our society today. We must not close our eyes to this suffering, whether it is in Rwanda, Bosnia, or anywhere else in the world.

While in Auschwitz on another occasion we came to the place where the camp commander was hanged at the end of the war. That evening in front of a group of people, many of whom were Jews, I asked: "What difference is there if we hang a Jew or the camp commander?" Because there is no difference. In both cases we are separating ourselves from the other so we can take a life. If we want to create a world where Auschwitz is not possible, we must behave differently from those who created it. This became very clear to me in that moment, standing in front of the gallows.

The human condition

As I've mentioned, the Pilgrimage for Peace and Life lasted eight months and covered twenty-one countries. I found that the issues that humankind faces, the way that suffering manifests itself, are not so different from country to country. We hold to the notion that people are a certain way because they are this nationality or that nationality, but we all share in the human condition. Selfishness, greed, unhappiness, depression, and alienation exist in all countries in very similar forms, and people attempt to deal with them in very similar ways—largely through distraction. Materialism presents one of the greatest distractions available. The more things I have, the less I must face myself. It is interesting to see how attached we can be to even the smallest things we own.

One of my most profound discoveries during this long pilgrimage was that the more affluent people were, the less they gave. And the less people had, the more generous they were. When we walked in Poland, people were extremely hospitable and generous. The hospitality began to diminish the closer we came to Austria, which is fairly affluent compared with Poland or the Czech Republic. When we walked in Cambodia, the generosity was incredible, though in a material sense they have far less than in Eastern Europe. No matter where we went in Cambodia, we were never without a place to stay, we were never without food to eat, we were never without water.

We had hoped to walk through Serbia, but those of us who had been granted permission were deported within twenty-four hours. In the United States we talk of the Serbs as villains, but the Serbs, in an absolute sense, are neither good nor bad; they are consumed by tremendous suffering and do not know what to do with this pain, and so it is acted out. We did go through Bosnia. We walked from Split to Mostar, where we stayed for six days.

We spent one day on the east side, praying, fasting, and singing, and many people joined us. We also had some problems. For our healing services we created an altar that included a statue of the Buddha and a crucifix, as well as some other objects. At one point a local man drove up, jumped out of his car, and ran toward the altar. He grabbed the statue of the Buddha and threw it to the ground, saying there was nothing higher than Allah. We bowed and continued to sing and to pray, then when he had gone, we cleaned the statue and put it back on the altar.

Shortly afterward another man arrived. He grabbed the crucifix and threw it to the ground. We bowed, smiled, and continued to chant. When he had gone we picked the cross up, cleaned it, and put it back on the altar. After about ten minutes, someone else came with a copy of the Koran and added it to our altar. After that, we had no more problems. This experience was difficult for us—challenging, painful, and frightening—and at the same time it was important that the people who had thrown down the Buddha and the cross had a place where they could express their suffering, because their suffering is immense.

I have been ordained by those who have died

At the end of May we arrived in Vietnam. It was the first time I had been back since the war. Arriving at the Ho Chi Minh City (Saigon) airport, the same airport I first landed in as a soldier, I saw that not much had changed: There were still armed soldiers and armored vehicles everywhere, only they were Vietnamese, not American.

When I got off the plane, I asked myself: "Why am I here? I have done everything I am capable of to heal myself and repair the destruction I have caused. Why am I here?"

The bureaucratic process at the customs desk was endless and sullen. When I touched the aloofness, the coldness of the Vietnamese officials, I also experienced my own fear, because when I looked at them I saw myself, too. I know this coldness, this distance. It is a wall that I erect between myself and others to protect myself, and it is illusion!

Looking the Vietnamese in the face, those armed soldiers wearing the red star and carrying machine guns, I saw the enemy. And I guessed that they saw the enemy when they looked at me, too. I could feel that I was becoming rigid, aggressive, goading; I was challenging them, questioning their bureaucracy, acting out my suffering. In that moment, I was living in forgetfulness. But my own actions became a bell of mindfulness that brought me back to my breath. When I placed my awareness on my breath, I became more and more rooted in the present moment and was able to be in direct contact with my suffering, so it did not control me. I did not have to act out my suffering through violence or aggression.

When I came back to my breath and looked again at the Vietnamese soldiers, I saw myself reflected. I saw myself again as a soldier in Vietnam, trained not to feel. Since becoming ordained, my task is to speak with those who have shut down in this way, to touch their suffering and the suffering they awaken in me. I find that my monastic vows empower and encourage me on this path.

While in Vietnam, I visited a place called Nha Trang, a city on the South China Sea that had not seen much direct fighting. Nha Trang had been a military headquarters for the Americans, a place where decisions were made concerning the war. I went there to sit in meditation and to breathe. I also went there to do a Zen Buddhist service that invites and feeds the hungry spirits, alive, dead, and lingering.

One night I was doing some walking meditation along the beach, breathing in and breathing out, and suddenly I felt very angry. Nha Trang is a beautiful place: There are elegant French colonial-style buildings, beaches of fine white sand, palm trees; the water is warm and intensely blue, and there are marvelous waves for surfing. I thought of the soldiers who had been there during the war, who had never experienced combat directly, had never been in the jungle, had never seen anyone die, never had to kill anyone, who always had enough to eat, and I felt intense anger.

"These people call themselves Vietnam veterans! They were on a vacation!" The emotion I touched was incredibly powerful, and it was extremely important for me to access these thoughts and feelings that had been bottled up for years. Until I can access these strong emotions, there is no chance that they can be healed. Until I am willing to see them, touch them, embrace them, these feelings will continue to control my life. What was hiding in the jungle was always more dangerous than what could be seen. Our emotions are the same. When we recognize our emotions and bring them to consciousness, they cannot ambush our good intentions, our desire to act with loving-kindness. As long as they lurk unseen, our intentions and our actions can never be trusted.

In addition to anger, for a long time I experienced a lot of guilt about having survived. How come I survived when so many didn't? Through the practice of mindfulness, my survivor's guilt, to a large extent, is being transformed into an intense sense of responsibility. Though in a technical sense I was ordained as a Zen Buddhist monk by Bernie Glassman, I have come to feel that I was also ordained by all those who have died. I feel an intense responsibility to everyone who's ever died in war, in any war. For every American soldier who died, for every South Vietnamese soldier who died, for every civilian who died, for every Vietcong soldier who died—for every person who's ever died in that war or any war, I feel an intense responsibility, because they are in me. An intense responsibility because I have been given the awareness, through the death of these people, through their sacrifice, that war and violence are never a solution.

Just walking

When I'm on pilgrimage, I've often been asked, "Why are you walking? What is your goal?" And I often respond by saying, "I'm walking just to walk." People have trouble getting their minds around that. It doesn't make sense. It may seem quite foolish. But the essence of the practice of pilgrimage, as I understand it, is walking just to walk. If I have an agenda, if I have a goal, then the unknown can't be my teacher, I can't really be in the present moment. When I'm consumed with accomplishing my goal, I can't see all the riches and wealth that life has to offer me in the present moment.

On the pilgrimage from Auschwitz to Vietnam, I went to practice peace, to be peace, but I was not walking expressly for peace. If I have some preconceived notion of what peace is, I might never be able to participate in it. Peace is not an idea, peace is not a political movement, not a theory or a dogma. Peace is a way of life: living mindfully in the present moment, breathing, enjoying each breath. Peace becomes. It is fresh and new with every moment.

When I walk, I meet and talk with people along the way. One of the things I talk about is healing and how it starts with one's self. As self heals, then healing begins to become manifest in the family, in the community. Like ripples of a stone you throw in the water. I had to face the implications of this for myself. The ripples of this pilgrimage would soon lead to another one.

The American Zen Pilgrimage

After the journey from Poland to Vietnam, I wanted to walk in Africa. As I began to talk about this pilgrimage, I was suddenly confronted with a powerful awareness. I had never walked in America. I needed to walk at home. When I was back in the States, I approached Bernie Glassman and said, "You know, I'm thinking about maybe, perhaps,

walking across America at some point. I don't know." I
left it at that, and we didn't talk any further about it.

When I came back to see him three weeks later, the
various priests at his center greeted me by saying, "Anshin, what a wonderful thing you're doing. This is incredible." And I said, "What? What are you talking about?"
They said, "The pilgrimage you're doing." So I went from
sort of, maybe, thinking about it to, in the thoughts of the
person who ordained me, actually doing it. At first I was
angry, because I had not yet made this decision, but by not
acting out of this anger, I was soon able to realize that it
was the push I needed. So I made the commitment. I was
just going to put on a pack and start walking. Right
through the middle of America.

We started from Yonkers, New York, on March 1, 1998,
and we reached Albany, California, on July 28, 1998. We began
our walk by going south down Route 9 (Broadway) through
Yonkers and the Bronx, then crossing into Manhattan. At
178th Street we climbed a set of steps and walked across the
George Washington Bridge, heading west. We had a lot of
company with us from Yonkers to 178th Street. We still had
a fair amount of company as we climbed the bridge. But
when we reached the midpoint of the bridge, only seven of us
continued on. Six of us intended to walk all the way to California. In the end, four of us completed the journey: Tobias,
Wiebke, Hamzha, and myself. Tobias is a German photogra-
pher, Wiebke is a German Zen student. They had both made
the commitment to walk the entire distance. Hamzha is a
man who lives homeless on the streets of Manhattan and was
connected with the Zen Community at Yonkers.

We walked directly through the center of the country,
through rural America. Between Hackettstown, New Jersey,

and Peoria, Illinois, the towns we stopped in had populations of about eighty to three thousand people. When we reached a town of three thousand, it seemed huge. We walked fifteen to thirty miles a day. We walked without money and without a support vehicle (until Boulder, Colorado, where we began relying on a truck to carry our water through the desert), and we carried everything we had on our backs. We walked whether it rained, whether it snowed, whether it was freezing cold or burning hot.

At the beginning of the pilgrimage, in the eastern states (New Jersey, Pennsylvania, Ohio), the police stopped us more frequently than in the middle of the country. We were stopped most often in Ohio. People called up the police to say, "You know, there are people walking on the road." It sounds funny that this would arouse suspicion, but in America people don't usually walk places. We walked for 150 days total. From the beginning we made no prearrangements of any kind. Each time we set out we had no idea what waited for us at the end of the day.

I could call this walk a cross-country alms prayer pilgrimage. In the Soto Zen tradition, the practice is called *takuhatsu*, alms begging. In this tradition we walk without money, asking for everything we need. In a traditional *takuhatsu* practice, you don't say anything; you simply stand in front of a place with your begging bowl and take whatever is given. I thought it a little more practical in this country to ask, because we could have stood in front of a church for days and people might not ever have understood why we were there. If we had not talked, we probably would have come in contact with the police even more frequently.

People don't commonly do this sort of thing in America. I know of a few people who have made various sorts of cross-country journeys—they've walked across, they've run across, and they've bicycled across. A woman who went by the name of Peace Pilgrim walked back and forth across the country for years. She wore a smock with a big peace sign on it and carried everything she owned in the pockets of her smock. She was supported by the generosity of the people she came in contact with. That was her life. But spiritual pilgrimages are rare.

Pilgrimage as spiritual practice is quite common in Asia and Europe. It's a powerful practice, and it's challenging to describe the nature of the learning one experiences to someone who has never been on one. There is no escape from the nature of your suffering in this practice. When you walk, you are constantly confronted with your self, your attachments, your resistance. You are confronted with what you cling to for the illusion of security. And in this practice, if you continue to cling to those things, it is sure that you will pay a heavy price. You'll be in a constant state of unhappiness because you'll always be fighting with the practice, attempting to control it in some way. During a pilgrimage, your attachments can also hurt you physically. It is often easy to determine how much suffering (emotional, psychological) a person is carrying by the amount of unnecessary things they carry in their backpack and how desperately they want to hang on to these things even at the cost of physical injury in the form of blisters, back strain, shin splints, and so forth.

The whole purpose of this practice is to let go—to let go of all expectations, all attachments, and just deal with what is presented in the moment. Living in this way is living the reality of life, living in the unknown, allowing the unknown to become our teacher. If you don't have a place to stay, if you are not provided food to eat, then you must deal with that reality.

When we arrived in a town, we would approach the various religious institutions and ask them for a simple place to stay and some simple food to eat. As you may guess, there are not many Buddhist institutions between New York and Denver, so we knocked on the doors of whatever religious institutions we found. We gave all of them the opportunity to live out their teachings. We didn't discriminate. We knocked on all their doors, accepting the proposition that if everyone said no we would sleep outside and we would not eat. Did that happen? You bet, though it didn't happen as often as I thought it would, and it didn't happen in the places that I thought it might.

Ohio was the most difficult state that we walked in. In the more than two weeks we spent walking there, only four churches opened their doors to us. But it wasn't the only state where we were turned away. In one town in Pennsylvania, all the churches said no in the middle of a freezing rainstorm that was turning into snow. We ended up sleeping outside in a pig barn at the fairgrounds. And it was one of the most wonderful nights we had. I was so thankful for that shelter. Luckily, we didn't have to share it with pigs; they were all gone. It was also an important night for us because until that point we had been receiving shelter and food on a consistent basis, and we began to take these gifts for granted. So here, when everyone said no to us, the suffering began to rise. The people in our group went into a panic. There was indignation and self-righteousness. The suffering began to get projected onto members of the group. People were arguing, becoming sullen, withdrawn, testy. Yet through this process we learned how important it is not to take one breath for granted.

The Buddha taught about the suffering created by our attachments—our attachments to form, to ideas, to things—and he taught about the importance of letting go of attachment. The pilgrimage provided us with a daily opportunity to realize this teaching. Just the reality of the walking itself presented us with an opportunity to explore attachment and nonattachment. We walked in subzero temperatures, so cold that the water bottles in our packs froze. I carried a jar of arnica, an herbal tincture for sprains, and it turned to paste. We walked through the deserts of Nevada in temperatures well over a hundred degrees. But interestingly, in the most extreme conditions, we walked the longest distances. In the desert we often walked thirty miles a day. And we were able to do it with joy. I believe that we were able to walk these distances because of our conditioning—physical, mental, emotional, and spiritual. Once we walked four miles in fifty minutes. That's quite a good pace, especially carrying a pack and climbing from, say, four thousand feet to seven thousand feet over a ten-mile stretch. The pace alone presented us with an opportunity to be powerfully aware of our breath—we really knew we were breathing. That pace put us right in touch with our breath, our resistance, our attachments, our limits. If you think you have no attachments or no expectations when you come to join a pilgrimage like this, the process quickly shows you the truth.

At one point we arrived in a Colorado town of about eighty people, with one church. Wiebke knocked on the door of the church to ask for food and shelter. What we didn't realize was that we had already met the pastor of the church. He was at the gas station grocery store when we first arrived in town and were attempting to figure out what to do next. So when Wiebke knocked on the door of the church and introduced herself, described our pilgrimage, and asked for help and support, the pastor said, "You're Buddhist. We won't help you out."

We were hot and tired from walking, so we went to the park in the center of town to rest. While we were resting there, a car pulled up. It was the pastor and his wife. He got out of the car, carrying some paper bags. These turned out to be bags of food for us. He wouldn't allow us to stay in the church, but he brought us food. Somehow he was able to transcend his own fear and insecurity—his own suffering—to help in the manner he could.

But in the course of our conversation in the park, he told me that I was the Antichrist. He was serious. I looked at him and said, "You know, I don't think so." He said, "Do you believe in Jesus Christ?" And I said, "Absolutely." I said this without blinking an eye, because it's the truth. I really admire and respect the teachings of Jesus. The pastor's next question was, "Have you accepted Jesus as your personal lord and savior?" And I said, "No, I haven't." He said, "You see, you're the Antichrist. If you don't accept Christ as your savior, then you're the Antichrist."

At that point in our conversation I asked, "How old are you?" He told me his age, and then I said, "Did you serve in the military?" He responded with, "Well, yes, I did." I said, "Did you serve in the Korean War?" He said he had. "What branch?" I asked, and he replied, "I served in the Navy." "You know, I served in the military also," I said. "I

served in the army in the Vietnam War." He said, "Isn't
America a great place that we can serve to protect. I served
so that you can do what you are doing." And I said, "Thank
you very much, and I understand that I served so that you
can do what you are doing." And I bowed to him.

We found a place where we could connect. That's what
I focus on—not the places that make us different, but the
places where we touch. Can I really look at people on the
street and know that I am not different from them, that
they are part of me, as close to me as my own family? There
is a widely practiced Buddhist meditation for cultivating
compassion that involves envisioning others—including
perfect strangers and even those you hate—as your own
mother. (If you have difficulty with your mother, you can
imagine that they are your child or another loved one.) It is
possible to meet people who you once thought were different or frightening and discover the places where you touch:
the places where you both share the human experience of
suffering and joy.

I won't deny that when the pastor called me the Antichrist, one of the first things I experienced was anger. And
then I felt hurt. I vacillated between wanting to punish
him in some way and then wanting to convince him of the
wrongness of his position, to engage in debate with him.
But none of those responses would have been productive. I
look for the places where we touch. The place of interconnectedness. Because if I see the other as separate from myself, that's when I involve myself in the cycle of suffering,
when I start to act out from my suffering. The result is a
spiral of anger, hatred, violence, war. We are either making
friends or making enemies every day of our lives.

Of course when somebody calls me the Antichrist,

feelings of anger are likely to rise up in me. But if I act out of this place, then who am I? If I try to elevate myself above him, I've made myself theologically superior. And I've lost sight of the pure truth that I'm not different from him. In fact, I have the same impulses that he does. So I use my awareness not to separate myself from him but to simply bear witness to what arises in me when I encounter such aggression, fear, and narrowness of vision. And then I breathe and look for the places where we touch.

The fear and aggression that we experienced on our walk across America were genderless and ageless. It came from men, from women, from children, from older people, from young people. We experienced it across the board. And the generosity that we experienced was also genderless and ageless. We had both experiences.

We give just to give

I'd estimate that for every five religious institutions that we approached, four said no. But we also experienced some spontaneous acts of generosity. In one town we had been turned away by all the religious institutions and other helping institutions. So Wiebke asked two women walking down the street if there was a Quaker meeting house in the area. We learned that there was a Friends meeting house about two or three miles away. We had just walked eighteen miles in eighty-five-degree weather, and, attached to my exhaustion, I said, "I'm not walking any more." One of the women said, "I have some neighbors who are Buddhists, and maybe they would let you stay with them. Why don't you come home with me and then we'll go over and ask." She brought us to her house and prepared a meal for us. Then she brought me to the neighbors, who immediately said yes. In fact, they were overjoyed that we had come along. They felt privileged to host us.

About halfway through the pilgrimage, to make our journey more manageable, when we were ready to leave a town we would ask for a ride ten miles out of town, leaving us only fifteen to twenty miles to walk to our next stop. In one Kansas town, the priest asked the congregation to help us, but no one came forward, so he called the Methodist minister, who was willing to give us a ride. He arrived at ten minutes to seven in the morning with his secretary, and during the drive he was so moved by what we were doing that he took it upon himself to organize the rest of the state for us. So from that point forward we had places to stay in Kansas. We didn't know him, we didn't spend much time together. He just responded to us in this way.

Another time we asked a woman living alone on a farm whether we could sleep in her barn. "No, I couldn't let you stay in the barn," she said. "Come sleep in my house." She invited seven absolute strangers walking on the road into her house. This is the actualization of what the Buddha taught as the *dana paramita,* or the teaching of selfless giving. As I understand this teaching, it is not what we give or how much we give but the intention with which we give that matters most. That we give just to give, whatever it is—a smile, a handshake, a bow—that we give selflessly.

Bringing the teachings to life

One of the things that drew me to Zen Buddhism and enables me to stay connected to this spiritual path is the fact that it doesn't have a strong history, particularly in the

United States, of missionizing or proselytizing. For me, Zen Buddhism is about staying focused and concentrated with self and healing. When I go to an area of intense suffering, I don't go there to convert anybody to my way, but I do practice my tradition when I'm there. As much as possible, I seek to embody the teaching, to bring the teaching to life.

In the walk across America, others often proselytized us. It was important for us to stay open and respect the teaching of others. In Saint Joseph, Missouri, we were hosted by a family from what they called a "nondenominational church." In my experience, any church in the United States that calls itself nondenominational is usually an evangelical Christian church. They actually have a very precise perspective on the Bible and on religion. This family brought us into their home, fed us, and then invited us to attend church with them. And it turned out to be a wonderful experience, because I said, "We're glad to come and stay with you, we're glad to come and experience everything you have to offer us, but please don't proselytize us. We are committed to our practice, and this is what we want to do." And they respected that. I was introduced to all the deacons in this church, and it was a rich experience, an opportunity for me to grow and learn.

Knocking on the door of a full-gospel evangelical church was usually a wonderful learning experience. When I'm on pilgrimage, I walk in the traditional clothing of my monastic lineage: I wear my *koromo* (a long black tunic), my peacemaker vest (a black vest with colorful brocade), my *rakasu* (my daily robe, a traditional garment in Zen Buddhist traditions worn around the neck that looks like an oversized pouch). I carry a backpack, and my head is shaved. Basically, the pastor who comes to the door encounters a bald-headed guy in a dress. And with my walking stick, I must look a bit like Merlin without the hat.

I would say, "My name is Claude Anshin Thomas and I'm a Zen Buddhist monk. We're on an alms prayer pilgrimage, we're walking without money, and we're looking for a simple place to stay and simple food to eat. Is it possible for you to help us?" Some would say, "You're Buddhist? There's no way we can help you." In this moment of rejection they provided me with a perfect opportunity to embody my practice. I would place my hands together and bow (in the traditional manner of my lineage, called *gassho*), thanking them for hearing our request, and then we would move on.

I took these occasions as an opportunity to bear witness to any anger that arose in me, without becoming trapped in it, or reacting from it, but instead bowing to this person because in that moment this person is my teacher. He or she is giving me the opportunity to really see and experience what keeps me from living in my awakened nature.

In each place we stopped, we invited people to come to our services. Pastors, priests, nuns—people from all sorts of backgrounds—attended our services. We were once invited into a full-gospel evangelical church on the last day of a five-day revival. We sat there while they were playing music and hallelujah singing—it was quite intense. Then the preacher stood up before the whole congregation and said, "We have some people here, they're Buddhist, and they're walking across the country. You should pay attention to them. You can learn from them, because they are demonstrating and living a commitment to faith. You could benefit from what they're doing." When he said this

I just broke down and cried. This man got it. He understood, and he really embodied his own spiritual teaching. He was not an ideologue. He was not preaching a gospel of alienation and fear. In that moment, joy just rushed through me, and I was able to receive this gift. I thanked him and his congregation afterward. It was a very unusual experience.

We had the opportunity to put our altars up in a lot of Christian churches and to do our services there. We also had the opportunity to do services in some very difficult places. Two counties that we walked in were heavily populated by members of the Ku Klux Klan. We were a pretty diverse group—men and women, different colors, the bald-headed guy in a dress—but never once did we get harassed or bothered. Not once. And we did our practice outside; we did this practice everywhere, we didn't hide it. It was important to let the bell of mindfulness sing, really let it sing.

Sangha is the entire spectrum of the universe

One of the core Buddhist teachings is the concept of sangha, or community. Sangha is the entire spectrum of the universe, because the entire universe exists here, now. It is also my immediate community, the people I am practicing with. Without the community of people walking with me, without their presence, the walking would have been more difficult. There were days I might not have walked if I hadn't been responsible for getting the others up and out on the road. So their presence empowered me; it helped me to focus.

Anyone can come with me on a pilgrimage. It's not necessary for a person to become a student of mine or to spend time with me to learn this practice. It is open. People learn about my work through the various talks and retreats that I facilitate. When I made the commitment to do the walk across America, I simply announced to people that I was going to do it. I extended a general invitation to anyone who wanted to walk with me. They just needed to understand the terms: You walk without money, you carry everything on your back, and we walk twelve to thirty-seven miles a day.

If you'd asked Hamzha, Tobias, and Wiebke, when we took the first step in Yonkers, whether we would make it to California, I think they would probably have said, "I don't know, but I don't think so." Because if you think about the whole trip, approximately four thousand miles, your mind will likely tell you that you can't walk that far. But if you just walk one step after another, the process is much more manageable. It's like the practice of sitting meditation. If I commit myself to fixed ideas about posture, how long I'm going to sit there, and so forth, I may miss the point, and that is just sitting. My commitment need only be sitting just to sit. I can walk just to walk. I can eat just to eat. I can breathe just to breathe. This is waking up. There isn't necessarily a limit to a pilgrimage. There may be a point at which the walking ends for some, but the journey to wake up can be one step, it can be a thousand steps, it can be the journey of a lifetime.

Walking in Germany

I went on another pilgrimage in 1998, this time through Germany. I walked with the focus of visiting as many sites of suffering from the Second World War as possible and to bear witness to the continuing effects of that war. What I hadn't anticipated was that I would encounter sites of suffering from countless periods of violence throughout European history.

On this pilgrimage there were six people who walked the entire distance, which was about seven hundred miles, and twenty-five to thirty people walked with us for some portion of the time. In the retreats and services that we did at the various sites of terror, abuse, degradation, torture, and killing, about two hundred people in total participated.

The experiences of this pilgrimage, the depth of it, are still so close to me, so dense, that I find it difficult to fully comprehend or process. We visited concentration camps where millions of Jews were exterminated; Buchenwald, where more than sixty thousand people were killed; Theresienstadt, where tens of thousands were killed; Ravensbrück, where untold thousands were worked to death; and Hadamar, a mental institution where more than sixty thousand people (predominantly German nationals) were euthanized in a seven-year period. After the war, many of these camps were used by the Soviets to imprison, interrogate, and torture Germans who had been identified as Nazis. As a result, tens of thousands more died in some of these camps.

And these are just a few of the places we could have visited, the camps being simply the conclusion of a process that began long before their conception. The process that led to the creation of places like Auschwitz continues to exist in our own contemporary social structures and in the social structures of other countries throughout the world. Through my witnessing I have been brought to the awareness that the process that led to these atrocities, this terror, is insidious and pervasive. Its seeds are rooted in the very nature, the very fabric of what is commonly accepted as civilization.

I was also increasingly sensitized to the reality that the policies of the National Socialist German Workers Party (NSDAP), or Nazis, could not have been carried out without the complicity of the countries and societies of Europe (as well as the rest of the world). These policies could not have been enacted without the intense collective denial of German society and the collective denial of the world society. The planning and initiation of this system of abuse, exploitation, torture, and terror, the politics that enabled it to be carried out, were not a secret. All of this was taking place quite in the open, on the world stage.

This pilgrimage also made me more sensitive to the dangers of self-righteousness. Self-righteous action is based on the projection of one's own suffering onto external sources (people, places, and things). This sort of projection-based decision making is dangerous at whatever level it takes place, and unless we are rigorously committed to looking at the entire, detailed construction of the events that led to the killing of more than fifty-five million people during this period of world history (1939–1945), this cycle will continue to repeat itself again and again. We have witnessed this in the Stalinist Soviet Union, the Maoist Chinese Cultural Revolution, Pol Pot's Cambodian Khmer Rouge; in the early attempts by the United States to eradicate the Native Americans; and even in the continued use of the death penalty as an accepted means of punishment. As I witnessed during this pilgrimage throughout these sites of terror and abuse, laws can quickly become enacted to expand the net and increase the field of qualification for extermination.

We see the results of this kind of righteousness in the ongoing attempts to eradicate indigenous populations throughout the world, in the events in the Balkans and Rwanda, and also in the destruction of the environment. Witnessing the continuing cycle of suffering, I often feel overwhelmed, fearful, and so powerless. I ask myself over and over, "So, what can I do? What is the proper response?"

Throughout this pilgrimage through Germany, we visited the sites of synagogues that were destroyed during on the night of November 9–10, 1938 (Kristallnacht, "the Night of Broken Glass"), and did services. We visited the Jewish cemeteries that were still in existence and did services. We visited former prisoner of war camps and did services on the sites of mass graves. We visited mental hospitals that were used as euthanasia centers and did services in the gas chambers and killing rooms. We visited former Gestapo headquarters and did services; we visited former sites of Jewish schools and did services; we visited the collection points for Jehovah's Witnesses, homosexuals, Sinties and Romanies (Gypsies), and political prisoners and did services. We stayed in churches that had made deals with the NSDAP (Nazis) and turned a blind eye to what was happening, churches that had been complicit with the policies of repression, torture, and extermination, and we did services.

We engaged people at all levels of the social structure and invited them to talk with us, to tell us their stories so that we could listen and learn. We visited with Jewish communities that were rebuilding themselves. We spoke with skinheads (the new fascists), engaging all those who would talk with us. We listened to their stories and responded when asked. We responded from a place of bearing witness: We didn't judge the speakers, or rather, we paid close attention to the judgments that were rising in us and simply did not act from these judgments. We sought to listen deeply and to understand their suffering.

What I also became aware of on this pilgrimage was that I don't know what I would have done if confronted with the kind of choices that others were controlled with in the face of National Socialism. What I do know is what I did when I was faced with these sorts of choices during the period of U.S. involvement in Vietnam. I volunteered to go into the military, I volunteered to go to Vietnam, and I killed and destroyed what I perceived as the other. I don't know what I would have done or how I would have acted in the camps had I been a prisoner. But I do know what I did when I realized that the propaganda I had been fed was not really the truth: I continued to fight, kill, maim, and destroy, rationalizing my actions as protecting others. Perhaps I would have been the prisoner in Buchenwald who choked another prisoner to death over potato peels.

Over and over, what I kept being confronted with on this pilgrimage is the complicity essential at all levels of the social fabric for such horrors to be enacted and carried out—how I have participated in such horrors and how subtly all this horror begins.

The question then arises, "So what is the appropriate response to these events in our daily living?" I can only say that for me the appropriate response is always one of zero tolerance. Zero tolerance at whatever level and scale I encounter such racism, discrimination, self-righteous action, or abuse of power.

The next question then is: "What are the skillful means or methods needed to reinforce and sustain this position?" The response that keeps arising in me is to live my life differently, to live the spiritual reality of life (the knowledge of our interconnectedness), to be uncompromising in this spiritual commitment, and to find whatever means available to support this path. Meditation, the process of knowing oneself intimately and deeply, is for me the core, because mindfulness is the only possible antidote to the mindlessness that leads to complicity with cruelty, violence, and genocide.

At its inception, the NSDAP movement was not taken seriously and for the most part went unchallenged. As I reflect on these circumstances, the only way that I can imagine such horror and terror going on unchallenged is that the governments of all the countries witnessing just couldn't admit their own guilt. To intervene, to speak up, to speak out, would have meant that they would have to individually and collectively in some way acknowledge their own participation, support, and initiation of like actions.

This becomes clear to me because of how I was trained and conditioned to establish my own position when confronted with violence or unhealthy behavior. I was trained not to speak up. On the surface this may seem like good advice. It is the easier path, the path of least resistance. I was trained not to question things, because if I did, this would set me apart somehow. But the real reason for not speaking up was that it would bring into focus my own similar behavior. The denial of my own behavior would become that much more difficult, if not impossible.

To do the work of peace, to live the spiritual reality of life, I have no choice but to acknowledge that at whatever the scale (individual, familial, social, or national), policies enacted from a perceived position of superiority will be exploitive, abusive, and dangerous. So I must look at where these seeds of superiority are in my life, see how they manifest themselves, and make a commitment not to turn away.

After we completed this pilgrimage through Germany, I traveled to Italy. In Portogruaro, located in northeastern Italy halfway between Venice and Trieste, I was invited to give a public talk, the title of which was "The Seeds of Violence, the Roots of War." I gave this talk to a group of schoolchildren from around the area. There were about three to four hundred students ranging in age from fourteen to eighteen. There was also a fairly large representation of teachers in attendance.

This was not my first visit here. I was invited for the first time in May 1999 as part of my trip to the war zone associated with the military actions that were being conducted in Kosovo and Serbia. I was invited to speak with these students about the nature of war because they were so deeply affected by this war effort, as were most of the people who lived in this area. Portogruaro is close to Aviano Air Base, the NATO facility from which a large portion of the bombing campaign was being conducted. Day and night they could hear the planes taking off and returning. Their proximity to war evoked the question, "So when are the bombs going to start dropping here?"

To deal with this question, I made every effort to help the students realize that the roots of this war resided also in them and in their families. I made efforts to help them to first identify these seeds of violence. I discussed the many faces of suffering, the roots of war, in a young person's life, such as physical, sexual, and emotional abuse; dependency on alcohol and other drugs; self-destructive behaviors such as anorexia or bulimia. I encouraged them to look honestly at their lives and at their families' lives to notice this suffering, and I also let them know that they could do something to change their understanding and their behavior, and therefore they could do something very concretely to bring an end to war.

I was taken by car from Portogruaro to Padova, where I visited what used to be the Jewish quarter. Before the rise of the Fascists in Italy and their alliance with the NSDAP of Germany, there was a thriving, relatively large Jewish community in Padova totaling about two thousand people. In April of 1943 all the Jews from this community were arrested, brought to a central point, and deported for extermination. The synagogues were burned. Two of the synagogues have since been rebuilt, but only one still functions as a synagogue. The other one is now a cinema.

Italy was not a friendly place during World War II if you were in opposition to the Fascist government or if you were Jewish or otherwise different. And Italy still has deep struggles with its past. For the most part I haven't encountered many Italians who are willing to deal with this part of their history very directly. It seems that there is a conscious or unconscious effort not to remember. This effort not to remember is reinforced by not talking about this period. And by not talking, the opportunities for healing are limited. When we miss these healing opportunities, as I know from my own life experience, the suffering gets recycled, passed on to succeeding generations, continuously acted out with less and less clarity about its sources. In my family, my father was a soldier, my grandfather was a soldier, my great-grandfather was a soldier.

During my travels in Italy, I was also reminded how aggression, rooted in fear and lack of awareness, generates a lot of self-deception. I could see this in the eyes of the people I spoke with when I asked them questions like "What did your parents do during the war?" While in Venice, I visited the old Jewish quarter. This community was established in the thirteenth or fourteenth century. Despite periods of deportations and persecutions, by the eighteenth century a permanent community had taken root and begun to flourish. But this community was cloistered, a ghetto. The entry points all had large wooden doors that were locked at night. On these wooden doors there was a sign that read: THESE DOORS ARE LOCKED FOR THE PROTECTION OF THE JEWISH COMMUNITY. But of course there's another reality to locked doors: Nobody can get out!

This reminded me of one of the stories that I had the privilege to hear while on pilgrimage through America. I heard this story from a Japanese American man, one of the many who spoke to us about their forced relocation to internment camps in the western United States during World War II. At one of these camps, this man asked American military personnel, "Why are we here?" The answer that came back was, "You are here for your own protection." He responded, "Then why are the guns pointed at us?"

During two separate incidences, one in 1943 and another in 1944, the Jews of Venice were arrested, brought to the central square of the Jewish quarter, and from there deported to the death camps. At this site I lit incense, did prostrations, and offered prayers of healing for the ghosts both in and out of this square. Sometimes I simply don't know what else to do.

I've learned a great deal about myself and about the human condition on pilgrimage. I've witnessed the universality of suffering, how we all share the same essential problems, and the devastating and long-lasting effects of violence and war. What leads me to continue my practice is the most profound sense of responsibility not to let any of the lives that have been lost in any war be wasted. Those lives have been sacrificed to help us to wake up to the senselessness of war. War is not something that happens externally to us. In my understanding and in my experience, it is a collective expression of individual suffering. If we want war stopped, then we must wake up.

I didn't know what to do for those I had killed in Vietnam until Thich Nhat Hanh taught me: "Just practice. Because when you walk, you walk for all those who have ever been abused, exploited, terrorized, crippled, maimed, or killed under any circumstance. When you walk, you walk for all veterans. When you sit [in meditation], you sit for all veterans. So you wake up, and as you heal, you heal them in you."

So when I walk, I walk for all victims of violence and aggression. When I walk, I walk for all veterans. For and with them all.

6

Finding Peace

In 1997 I was in Switzerland, traveling by train from Zurich to Winterthur. A young man entered the train, sat down across from me, and took out a pack of cigarettes. This section of the car was nonsmoking. I don't smoke, and I avoid being exposed to secondhand smoke if I can help it. I watched him take out a cigarette and put it in his mouth. At that point I simply said, "Excuse me," and pointed to the NO SMOKING sign. He stopped and looked at me for a brief moment; I could see that his mind was working. His body then assumed a defiant posture, and he went ahead and lit his cigarette.

I considered my options. I could take away the lighter, smash it on the floor, grab the cigarette out of his mouth, crush it in my hand, and punch him in the face—and then say, "You don't really want to light up another one, do you?" This is actually what ran through my head. Because I was dressed in robes, the next thought I had was that this was probably not the best thing to do. I could see the head-line in the newspaper: AMERICAN ZEN MONK BEATS UP MAN ON TRAIN. In that moment I stopped. My suffering had become manifest. I soon recognized that the anger I felt was a product of my own pain and conditioning, and he was not responsible for that. In fact, he gave me a great gift: the opportunity to see my mental habits more vividly. He was my bell of mindfulness.

I stopped and came back to my breath, breathing in and breathing out. As I watched him smoke his cigarette, I was able to say to him, "I'm sorry that you have to destroy your health in this way. I'm sorry that you are suffering so much," and I bowed to him.

We both got off the train at the same stop. I met the person I was visiting, and we got sandwiches and went to the park. As we sat and ate, I was telling him the story of the young man on the train, when I looked up and saw the same young man walking across the park with a young woman, perhaps his girlfriend. I invited them to come over and sit down. Although his companion seemed uneasy, they did sit down and we talked. I was able to say to him that despite his actions on the train, I could sense that he was a sensitive and caring man because of his willingness to talk with me here in the park, and I told him again that it made me sad to watch him harming himself by smoking. I also asked that if he continued to smoke in the future, would he please consider the fact that there are others around him who are affected by this. In this conversation I didn't want to impose my views upon him, and I didn't want to have his imposed on me. I went on to ask him if he could appreciate the aggressiveness of his actions and that by being aggressive he invited more aggression. Someone else might have responded differently than I did.

If I had been aggressive with the young man on the train, this conversation would not have occurred. My work today is to stand firmly and yet nonviolently in the face of conflict. The question then arises, How do we best address such situations? How do we manifest nonviolence in the midst of conflicts in our daily lives? There are no clear-cut guidelines or definitive answers. And if we look for answers outside ourselves, we won't find them. The best response also changes from situation to situation. Was I completely nonviolent in my interaction with this smoker? Did I avoid more subtle forms of aggression such as trying to change him or "teach him something" from a position of superiority? Maybe, maybe not. Changing is difficult— and often messy.

Over time I've come to understand clearly that my feelings don't come from an external source. They're present within me. This I can work with. I have to accept that everything I feel—anger, despair, confusion, everything— is mine. If I find someone else's behavior inappropriate, it's not my place to change them; in fact I can't. But what I can do is look at them as my teacher. That doesn't mean I don't sometimes have very strong thoughts and feelings regarding the actions of others. It doesn't mean that I don't want to sit down and lecture them on how they should behave. But my work is to notice, to pay attention to these thoughts, these feelings and perceptions—and not to react from them. If I use my feelings as a point of practice, just breathing in and out, and work with what comes up in me, without acting from it, then I will, with practice, come to know what to do. Life will show me.

Over time I've also learned that anger does not have to be expressed in a violent way. I can be angry with someone and express that anger in a mindful way, and then it passes through me, it doesn't stay so long. For years my anger took the form of rage; it was like a parasite, feeding off me, destroying me. Anger would come into my consciousness and stay for days, months, years. Now it lasts sometimes hours, sometimes minutes. It is not feeding off me anymore.

But one place that anger still comes to me a lot is while I'm driving a car. However, it used to be that when another driver would act in a way that I perceived as aggressive or selfish, my feelings would begin to boil, quickly and suddenly exploding into rage. I would be consumed. I would be in my car screaming, shaking my fist, sometimes even wanting to run the other driver off the road or crash into the person's vehicle. I was swept away by my rage.

Gradually, by living a life rooted in the practice of meditation and mindfulness, I began to move from a place of being out of control to a place of maybe just saying some not very friendly words and making some not very friendly gestures with my hands. These acts may seem pretty innocent, but they are still aggressive, and they water the seeds of violence. Now when I feel this sort of anger coming up, it becomes a bell of mindfulness, inviting me not to react in the moment. To stop, breathe, and become the observer. This, for me, is the essence of meditation.

With this practice of stopping and breathing, my anger does not go away; it will still be there, so another helpful tool is talking (the practice of mindful speech), talking about my feelings honestly with people I am close to. Maybe I need to talk for a day, maybe two days; maybe I will need to talk for twenty years. It doesn't matter. What is important is that I talk, that I share deeply that which keeps me trapped in suffering. And slowly, slowly, the anger dissipates. The rage is replaced with compassion. All the people driving on the road are suffering too, with their own wars. All these people, rushing and hurrying, cut off from one another within their armored personnel carriers, have so much in common with me, with each other. Have you ever noticed how much more difficult it is to be rude to another driver once you've establish eye contact?

In my practice and in my travels I have witnessed that there is little difference between our feelings of aggression and war. War is not something that happens externally, outside ourselves, in places like Bosnia or Kosovo; it is not something that happened in Germany sixty years ago or in Vietnam thirty years ago or is happening far away in Iraq or Afghanistan now. War and ag-gression happen every day, they are happening now, here. Think about this: Within a mile of where you are reading this book, you can be sure an act of aggression will be committed. Perhaps a child will be sexually exploited, a woman will be battered. Someone may be emotionally abused. People will have physical fights or shout angry words at each other. Perhaps someone is lying drunk and hungry and a passersby insults him. This is war. This is the nature of suffering.

Collectively, Americans have loathed and rejected Vietnam veterans because we are a painful reminder of the reality of human cruelty and aggression. Most Americans would rather we just go away, remain out of sight, so that they can go on believing that war and brutality are things that happen somewhere else among other kinds of people. And the experience of Vietnam, and many of us who fought in Vietnam, will not let our country forget that such war and aggression have deep and long-lasting consequences. That people cannot simply get on with life as usual. The veterans of the Vietnam War have helped our society to learn that there is really no such thing as the "greatest generation." In reality, every generation suffers, and every generation that fights a war must live with its profound and far-reaching consequences.

Why must we all suffer? Why does everyone have his or her own personal Vietnam? I don't ask why anymore; it is a pointless question. There isn't any answer. Suffering is in the world because it is in the world. Without suffering there is no joy, and I can't know what joy is without going through suffering. I also learn through spiritual practice, through meditation and supportive ritual, how to live with this reality, the reality of suffering. I learn not to hide from it. All the while the nature of healing, of transformation, begins to become more clear.

Our suffering is not our enemy

Society teaches us that suffering is an enemy. We are constantly encouraged to reject what is unpleasant, disappointing, or difficult. "What's all this suffering? Let's be happy! Have fun!" But our suffering is not our enemy. It is only through a relationship with my pain, my sadness, that I can reach the other side, that I can truly know and touch the opposite, which is my pleasure, my joy, and my happiness.

I often relate to my emotional suffering as though it were a physical pain. When I feel physical pain, society pushes me to take medication to relieve it, not to touch it, not to explore it or seek to understand it. I am conditioned to make every effort to avoid discomfort. I went through a long period of my life living from this conditioning. I took a lot of drugs, so many that I couldn't feel my physical pain or my emotional and spiritual pain—at the same time, it was also impossible for me to touch genuine joy, or healing, or anything at all. It was just impossible.

My body is covered with scars from my wars. Every time I look at my body, touch one of these scars, I touch again the reality of war, and when I touch the reality of war, I touch all the suffering that is intrinsic to war. In the past, when I felt pain from a scar, I tried to repress it, to hide it from myself. But the physical wounds are not the most significant wounds of war. The wounds of the soul, the spiritual wounds, the emotional wounds—they are far deeper, though less obvious. And they are much more unpleasant to look at.

Can I imagine a time in the future when these scars and these experiences will dissolve, drop away, so that I will finally be free? This is not actually a condition of freedom. I'm free right now. Because I can acknowledge that the scars are there. Because I no longer wish for them to be any different from what they are. Don't get me wrong, I spent a long time wishing that the scars of my life would just go away. But the more I wished for this, the crazier I felt. Because the reality is that my scars are part of me, like my own hand. I needed to learn to acknowledge them and to live with them in peace and harmony.

Earlier in this book I described how, after the war, whenever I heard a baby crying, I was sent into panic because of my experience with a booby-trapped baby in Vietnam. Now when a baby cries, I still experience fear, but I can begin to work with this fear in a different way. I can actually consider picking up a crying baby, and sometimes I do. I am living in a different relationship with my fear, no longer trying to escape it. When I wake up from a dream about the war, when I am in that space between sleep and wakefulness and I'm covered with sweat, for an instant I can still smell blood. For an instant I am unsure whether I am dreaming or the experience is real. Maybe the smells won't go away, maybe these sensations won't stop, maybe the screams of the dying won't leave me. But if I'm willing to look deeply into the nature of myself, embrace my suffering, and if I am rooted in spiritual practice, then maybe I can become more and more like still water. Through this process my relationship to these dreams will change, my relationship to the screaming will change, my relationship to the smells will become transformed—not gone, but transformed.

Recently I spoke with a man who said, "If you didn't feel things so deeply, if you were numb or if you were able to deny your feelings, you probably wouldn't have any trouble with the war." But in fact, the vast majority of the people who have closed themselves off from the reality of their experiences in war are suffering tremendously. Hiding or avoiding does not eliminate suffering, it just drives it more deeply underground. Then our suffering controls us more profoundly, in one form or another. We cannot hide from our pain. Trying to do so is like attempting to pour a liter of red paint into a half-liter container: It will spill and spread, covering every aspect of our lives.

That's what was happening to me when I hit bottom, a place where the pain was so intense I didn't know how to hold it. I thought my only option was to die. As we wake up to suffering, we may feel at some points as if we might explode. Because waking up to the boundlessness of suffering is intense, the pain is raw, the feelings immense—spaceless, formless, empty.

The practices of mindfulness and meditation have provided me with invaluable resources and tools in those moments, in those hell places. They also help me to be able to go to those places with others, to support them in caring for and healing themselves. I am able to sit with the dying, the wounded, encouraging them to tell their stories and listening deeply. I also go to the front lines and talk to soldiers about not fighting. I talk candidly with them about the effects and consequences of war. I am also able to go to the back wards of hospitals and mental institutions to visit the hidden casualties of war and listen to their stories. I sit with the disenfranchised, the social and cultural lepers, and listen. In all these places, with all these people, I practice breathing in and breathing out. I practice being fully present. And I offer them the tools of Zen Buddhist practice (direct experience), spiritual practice. I hope to help them discover the practices and tools that have helped save my life: sitting meditation, walking meditation, mindful speech, and deep listening. I also hope to provide the experience of sangha (community)— to demonstrate how community can support us on the path to healing and the path of awakening.

I invite people to bring an end to their isolation. Because together we can do more than we can alone. These tools, this practice of meditation, are important, even critical, because suffering is a reality of our lives, the lives of all of us. The "apocalypse now" is not just in Vietnam; it is not just for Vietnam veterans. It exists for all of us because we have all eaten the fruits of war, the fruits of violence, the fruits of hatred. If we don't wake up to this, it will destroy us. From the inside out it will destroy us. I know this from my own experience. And I know this because I observe this happening all the time.

War and trauma can be transformed

I am finding that the negative experiences of war and trauma can be transformed through an unwavering commitment to live mindfully. I have experienced this in a Buddhist monastery, on the streets, in war zones, at meditation retreats, and on my pilgrimages. I am finding that trauma can be transformed into more positive experiences. Life can be different. Though I have taken vows in the Soto Zen Buddhist tradition, which commits my life to this process, I am not special. Anyone can experience this transformation.

What it takes is a commitment, an unwavering commitment to live life differently, a commitment to changing our attitudes toward our suffering and bringing an attitude of nonviolence to our daily experiences and to our world. I don't want to kill. I don't want my son to kill. I want the violence to end. And yet preaching this won't help. We can only model this. We can't make the external world become peaceful; we can only become peace. This is the only way. There is so much trauma and sadness in the world, so much suffering. We need to be willing to look at it and at how we are responsible, how we contribute to this cycle. When we stop blaming others and begin looking deeply within ourselves, we can discover how suffering arises, how it is linked to violence, and how to stop the seemingly endless cycles of aggression.

This is not a process that happens overnight; I can't learn in one minute, or one day or one year, how to stop the suffering, although it is written in the Buddhist teachings that this is possible. "Sudden enlightenment," it is called. What my experience has shown me is a more gradual process, a process of learning. Learning through my mistakes, through my humanity. My experience has also shown me that waking up, that healing, is not a process of the intellect. It is not something that I can undertake with my thinking self. There is no book to read—not even this one. I must thrust myself fully into life. I must look deeply into my nature and awaken to my own suffering, my own pain, to begin to uncover and explore the nature of my experiences.

If I have to avoid my suffering in order to experience happiness, then this is not true happiness. It is not possible to be truly happy without touching our suffering, allowing it to be present in our lives. Learning how to hold it gently, like a child, to embrace it, to comfort it. And as we welcome this suffering in our lives, joy grows from this. This can happen now; this sort of transformation can happen right now. If we look deeply into the nature of our suffering, breathe into it with mindfulness, invite it into our lives, share it with others, then the possibility of transformation exists.

As a Vietnam veteran, I feel a responsibility to live, to heal, and to change. Veterans have this responsibility because we know war so intimately, so directly—and so that the lives of all those who have died in war will not be wasted. Their deaths ask us to learn, to see clearly that war, that violence in any form, is never a solution. That war and violence do not lead to peace. Their deaths then, in this respect, contribute to our healing, and as the war stops here, in us, war stops in the world. Imagine, if everyone stopped the war in themselves, there would be no seeds from which war could grow.

When I first heard Thich Nhat Hanh talk, I thought that I had to transform now, right this moment. If, in the course of a one-week retreat, I wasn't transforming garbage into roses, then I was a failure. In a conversation with me, he said: "You have begun the process of transformation, there is no telling how long it will take, but you must continue to water the seeds of sorrow and the seeds of suffering with mindfulness. To look deeply into the nature of yourself, to be willing to look honestly at those seeds that are within you and within each and every one of us."

The process of waking up can take a long time. During this process we must be forgiving of ourselves for the actions that we take in forgetfulness; we must be gentle with ourselves without being "lazy" or "excusing"; we must be disciplined and strong as well. We must be very committed to the act of waking up. If we act out of suffering, we must be able to forgive ourselves for that action but also be committed to not doing it again.

Our culture operates with the idea that healing means the absence of pain, but I've come to understand that healing doesn't mean that our pain and suffering go away. Healing is learning to live in a different relationship with our pain and suffering so it does not control us. The only way in which I can heal my wounds, the only way in which I can awaken, is to live in the present moment in mindfulness, breathing in and breathing out. Every time I come in contact with my fear, I first must learn to establish an open relation with it, neither attaching to it nor rejecting it, and then the next step is to see what is behind this fear. It's like turning over stones. I must continue to turn over stones until the day I die, looking ever more deeply.

There isn't any healing without vulnerability. We must be open to the reality of ourselves and not hide from anything. The way we discover the nature of our suffering is to step directly into life. Challenging ourselves, compassionately, at every turn. Really putting ourselves out there, being willing to make mistakes. That's where we learn about suffering and the way out of suffering.

Talking and listening

In the book *Achilles in Vietnam: Combat Trauma and the Undoing of Character*, Jonathan Shay, a psychiatrist, writes that recovery from combat trauma depends on communalization of that trauma—on sharing it. Sharing it with a community that can be trusted to listen, hold, and retell the story in an honest way.

When I was first suffering the trauma of the war, I didn't understand that I needed to tell my story, that I needed to talk about the experience, and keep on talking about it, because I had never been encouraged to do this. Anyone who has experienced trauma needs to talk about it, and we all have experienced trauma of some sort. I often hear people saying, "Oh, I could never talk about those things in my life. What would people think of me?" I guess those people are trapped in shame and guilt. They may feel there is some safety in keeping things hidden, but keeping all the pain to ourselves does not heal anything; instead it fosters abuse, abuse of self and of all sentient beings around us.

We are for the most part conditioned by our society and culture not to talk about our pain. But if we don't talk, if we don't create a language to express our feelings, healing will not take place. We will just continue to store up and re-create the cycles of suffering. The first step, which can be called a step into the unknown, is to begin to tell your story. What is helpful and necessary in this process is a safe container such as a community of like-minded people or a therapeutic environment. Becoming a Zen monk helped me to find and offer tools that aid in this process, helped me to find the tools to create and provide a container so that others who want to tell their stories can.

Let's listen to each other, really listen, without trying to change or fix anything. As we listen, let's just offer our openness and companionship. This is the beginning of the journey toward healing. Though we may think that we know how to listen, often when other people talk, we don't manage to really listen. We tend to judge what's being said, defend ourselves, react, offer advice, or seek to control the situation in some way. So a disciplined practice of listening will be helpful.

When I work with groups, I use the following exercise to cultivate real listening: We sit in a circle. An object —any object will do—is placed in the center of the group, and then we sit together for a few moments in silence focusing on the breath, on the rhythm of breathing in and breathing out. When someone in the group is moved to speak, the person silently signals to the group that he or she is going to pick up the object. (I often suggest that this person place the palms of the hands together in front of them, with the tip of the longest finger in line with the nose and bow, but in fact any gesture will do.) After completing the gesture, the speaker picks up the object and begins to talk, maintaining an awareness of the breath as an anchor.

While one person in the group is speaking, the others in the group just listen. The listeners also use the breath as an anchor, paying attention to the thoughts that arise, the feelings, and the perceptions. Listeners do not comment, give advice or suggestions, but just breathe in and out, seeking to listen deeply and also to notice what prevents or disturbs their ability to listen. When finished speaking, the speaker gestures to the group in some way, perhaps in the same way as when picking up the object, and places the object back in the center of the group. At this point the one who has been speaking becomes an active listener. What is said in these groups must stay within the group so as to maintain a sense of integrity and safety. It is also absolutely important to understand that such groups are not discussion groups and so at no point is there to be any cross talk. This is a disciplined practice that can foster active listening.

In emphasizing the value of speaking and listening, I want to point out the importance of realizing that healing doesn't happen to someone who has suffered trauma, it happens *by* someone who has suffered trauma. In our society we come to learn that something outside heals us—a physician, a therapist, a preacher, or God, if you will. The Buddhist perspective is that we are responsible for our own healing. We need tools to help us on our path, and they are rooted in spiritual practice, rooted in the truth that we cannot hide from our suffering or eradicate it.

There's a lot of projection that tends to go on when we suffer. We think that people or things outside ourselves are the causes of our suffering or the source of its relief. Our mind tells us that if we eliminate the perceived source of the suffering, then it will be gone for good. In war this process is cultivated and manifests in violence. Once embarking on this path, we become trapped in it; the violence controls us, creating a vicious circle that continues unchecked until we stop it by taking responsibility for our pain—by finding the courage to feel it, to enter into it, and not just to pass it on. If I don't look deeply into the nature of suffering, war continues. I must realize and accept that war has consequences on my life. I must accept the suffering that war infects me with. I need to learn how to embrace it so that I may clearly recognize its face as it creeps into the fabric of my life so as not to be controlled by it. And when it arrives, it is up to me to choose how to act in relation to it. The decision is mine. We may not have been able to control the trauma we have experienced, but we can take an active role in its healing.

The journey back to my son

I left my son, Zach, when he was three years old, and I was absent from his life until he was eight. My life during that period was increasingly chaotic and desperate, with increasing drug and alcohol use, violence, and sexual promiscuity. I believe my absence probably saved my son from a great deal of damage, but I also know he suffered because of it. When he was eight years old, I moved back to the town he lived in, but I was unable to develop any sort of loving, supportive relationship with him because I was still trapped in my suffering and not aware that I could do something to change my situation. But it was because of my longing to be connected with him and my sense of responsibility as his father, however distant that call was, that I felt a need to do something different with my life.

He was about eleven years old when I entered into treatment for drug and alcohol addiction. At that time I committed myself to doing everything possible to heal, to see clearly the causes and conditions of my life. I knew that I needed to look deeply into myself to understand what prevented me from being the father that my son deserved: a man who is emotionally present, intimate, loving.

As I began to change, my relationship with my son started to develop and deepen. From the time that my son was eleven until he graduated from high school, I made every effort to connect with him. I tried to become a supportive and positive influence in his life, and this was difficult because I carried so much guilt for having abandoned him. After I moved to Massachusetts, I drove back to Pennsylvania as often as I could to visit him. I remember how hard it was for me to leave him, and how hard it was for him to have me leave. Often, just before I had to go, he would manage to disappear, and so I just wouldn't leave. I would wait and wait until he came back so that we could do the difficult, painful, and important work of saying goodbye.

He would also come to me for visits during Thanksgiving or around Christmas, and I treasured these opportunities. These were also challenging times, however, because I didn't want to be just a person he had fun with, sending him back to his mother, who was the primary caregiver and disciplinarian in his life. I didn't want to be the "fun parent" out of respect for him and out of respect for his mother, who worked so hard and was so committed in providing him a stable foundation from which he could grow.

At a certain point when he was a teenager I told him that I would like very much for him to come and spend a year with me. His response was no. I was very disappointed, and yet I accepted it. His choice made sense. He simply didn't want to be separated from his friends.

During his junior or senior year in high school, he and I started to become closer. I think this was because he had questions that his mother just couldn't answer, and it was also at this point that his mother remarried and he had a great deal of difficulty with that. I had been preparing for this opportunity, unknowingly, with all the emotional, psychological, and spiritual work I had been doing. I was finally in a position to provide him with the support that he deserved. Though this was a challenging time, I believe I was able to be the father that he needed during that period of his life.

It was during this time that he told me he wanted to become a pilot, and he asked me how and where to learn. In this way, the question of whether he would serve in the military entered our relationship directly because, of course, in the military he could learn to fly. Despite everything I had been through, I didn't want to make this decision for him. I made every effort just to give him the information I had so that he could make his own informed decision. It was a great challenge for me not to try to control him, but I remembered how my father had handled my choice between going to college or going into the service. I wanted to make sure it was different for my son.

After he entered college he began to spend more and more time with me. We traveled together and shared many wonderful (and difficult) moments. I taught him to ride a motorcycle and we took several trips together. We camped, climbed, and did some sports together. He lived with me during his summer breaks, so we cooked together, did laundry together. We were sharing more of the practical sides of life, not just the fun things.

During this period I often asked him how he was affected by my leaving him. I asked because I was sure he had been affected by it, and I didn't want to avoid this topic just because it was difficult. His response was that for him it was no big deal and, while I knew that this was likely not the case, I had to practice restraint and just accept that for now this was what he could say to me about it. But I was also frightened that if he couldn't talk about this emotional wound he might end up repeating some, if not all, of the terrible realities of my life. But I also saw that I had to carry this fear; I had to allow it to be there and not act out of it. I couldn't push, demand, or attempt to preempt the possibility that he was shutting down emotionally, the way I had, and this was at times very, very difficult.

Over the years my son and I went to see a therapist together, and for a time he was in therapy himself. This was extremely beneficial. During one of our sessions, an important truth came to light: My son was able to express that he did not have as much difficulty with my absence as with my presence. This was of course difficult to hear. He had gotten used to me being gone. It was my return to his life that was hard for him to handle. But it was important for this to come out, for me to hear and understand this so that our connection could deepen.

While the transitions we have experienced in our growth together have not always been easy, we have been able to navigate them safely and our relationship has grown closer and closer. In his late twenties my son decided to pursue his childhood dream of learning to fly. At this writing he has completed much of the training that will enable him to pursue a career in flying, outside of the military. Watching my son move through his life, I'm filled with admiration for him. While I do not always agree with or support his choices, I respect the process he goes through. He is intelligent, kind, thoughtful, sensitive, and caring. He is a wonderful human being and a loving son. I am thankful every day to know him and to be a part of his life.

Peace is not the absence of conflict

Thich Nhat Hanh has said, "We need peace very much, but in order to bring peace, you have to be peace." But what is peace? My understanding of peace is always evolving. I've seen that if we have a fixed notion of peace, we lock ourselves into a very narrow, limited perspective, and we become so attached to it that we will not see the potential for peace existing in any moment. Peace is not fixed and rigid; it is organic, ever changing with circumstances and situations.

Though my understanding of peace continues to grow and change, I do know that peace is not the absence of conflict; it's the absence of violence within conflict. To settle conflicts requires that we touch aggression, touch anger, touch violence, but that we do not surrender to these qualities within us—this is what I have learned (and am still learning). We can and must learn how to be in disagreement with each other. Conflict will exist; what matters is how we address it. When we enter into conflict, we come face-to-face with suffering, our own and others'.

In conflict, if we make others responsible for our suffering rather than taking responsibility for it ourselves, the conflict will most likely not be resolved, and it will probably escalate—taking the form of violence and aggression.

We don't have to live in violence. I know that from my own experience. If we really want to live differently, we can. It is not a question of politics but of actions. It is not a matter of improving the political system or correcting social injustice. These are valuable but will not alone end war and suffering. We must stop fighting the endless wars that rage within. Engaging in this process, I have begun to heal from the wounds of the many wars that I have fought in: in my family, in school, in society, with alcohol and drugs, in Vietnam. I know now that I can practice peace by being peace. That's what became clear to me through my experience at the Buddhist monastery in France, when I was living with those I had perceived to be my enemy.

When I lived in Concord, Massachusetts, I rented a small one-room cottage. This cottage was the only real home that I have known. This house supported me, functioning as my hermitage, the place where I felt safe and could retreat to when my tentative relationship with the world—which I often perceived as hostile, inconsistent, and insensitive—was just too much for me. Most of the transformative experiences I've had that have enabled me to learn to live in a more integrated way with my suffering took place with the support of that cottage, the secure place where I felt at home. I had felt unsafe for so long in my life. This security was essential to my process of healing.

As I've mentioned before, I suffer from a disturbed sleep pattern that has been a part of my life since a nighttime attack in Vietnam in 1967. Since that time, I haven't slept for more than two consecutive hours in any one night. For years I fought against this fact. You see, my inability to sleep became a symbol to me of how I was no longer "normal," a constant reminder of the war that wouldn't leave me alone. I so much wanted my life to be different from the way it was. My sleeplessness became the central symbol of my not-all-rightness, of my deepest fears that I would never be all right.

On the rare occasions when I could get work, I was not able to hold the job because I just couldn't function as well as people who sleep at night. I was usually tired and distracted, and sometimes I simply couldn't get myself to work on time, because the early hours of the morning had become the only time that I was able to fall asleep.

Part of the reason I had difficulty sleeping was because of my night terrors: the sounds of artillery (that isn't there) firing in the distance, of helicopters on assault, that special look of everything illuminated by artificial light, the sounds of small arms fire, of the wounded screaming for a medic. For me, this is what rises up out of the silence that is special to night. I hated the sun going down. I fought and struggled with my inability to sleep, and the more I fought, the more difficult the nights became. So I turned to alcohol and other drugs (legal and illegal) for relief, but my suffering just got worse.

After I went through drug and alcohol rehabilitation in 1983, I stopped turning to intoxicants (the obvious forms). Looking back, this is probably the single most important event in my life, because it gave me the opportunity to experience my own life and to experience it directly—the only place from which healing and transformation can begin to take place.

Some years after getting sober, I was standing at the kitchen sink in my cottage in Concord, washing dishes. Above the sink was a window through which I could see a row of fifty-foot-tall pine trees that lined the driveway. That day as I did the dishes, I was watching a squirrel busy doing whatever it is that squirrels do, when I had a powerful experience. A voice inside me, the voice of awareness, said to me, "You can't sleep, so now what?" I began to laugh. It was a moment of complete acceptance. I finally understood that I just was how I was. To resist, to fight, to attempt to alter the essential nature of my life, was in fact making matters worse, and now I understood that I simply needed to learn how to live with the reality of who I was. In this moment I discovered that it was here, in the midst of suffering and confusion, that healing and transformation can take place, if I can stop trying to escape.

But I'm not special, you know. You can do this, too. You can face your own sorrow, your own wounds. You can stop wanting some other life, some other past, some other reality. You can stop fighting against the truth of yourself and, breathing in and breathing out, open to your own experience. You can just feel whatever is there, exploring it, until you also discover the liberation that comes with stopping the struggle and becoming fully present in your own life. This is the real path to peace and freedom. You could do this for yourself; you could do this for your family. Our whole world will benefit.

Beginning Meditation Practice

Here are descriptions of some basic meditation practices you can use in your everyday life. I've had the opportunity to teach meditation in a wide variety of settings to people from a lot of different backgrounds. Wherever I go, I teach the Zen Buddhist practices that have helped me to transform my life. You may not choose to take up all of these practices, but I encourage you to make the effort to engage them and find what helps you to develop greater awareness, openness, and compassion.

Sitting Meditation

Each morning and each evening practice sitting meditation for at least five minutes. Find a comfortable, quiet place and, if you like, put up a small altar with a candle, incense, and some flowers. You can sit in a chair or on the floor. When you sit in a chair, place your feet flat on the ground and sit upright (don't lean against the back of the chair). If you sit on the floor, you can sit cross-legged in the full- or half-lotus position, using a cushion to lift up your bottom so that your knees can more easily touch the ground. Or you can sit in *seiza* (the position that is frequently used among the monastic and lay practitioners in Japan), meaning kneeling and sitting on your heals. This position can be difficult for the beginner, so it may be helpful to place a cushion or meditation bench under your bottom.

Sit with your head erect and your chin tucked in slightly. Put your shoulders back. Visualize your ears being aligned with your shoulders and your nose aligned with your belly button. Find a comfortable position for your hands, such as resting them on your lap. Or you could take the more traditional approach of placing the fingers of your left hand on top of the fingers of your right hand, palms up, with thumbs almost touching. If you choose this position, hold your hands just in front of your navel. You can sit with your eyes open or closed. If you leave them open, lower your gaze, pick a spot on the floor in front of you, and let your eyes rest there. In sitting meditation, correct posture is important for many reasons, including the fact that it facilitates easy flow of the breath.

From this posture, focus on your breath, each in-breath and each out-breath. Feel your abdomen expanding when you breathe in, feel it contracting when you breathe out. There is nothing to be accomplished, nothing to be gained. Notice your thoughts, feelings, and perceptions. Don't attach yourself to them and also don't reject them. Just observe them and keep breathing. If you discover that you are having difficulty staying focused on your breath, use the technique of counting your breaths as a support. Take one in-breath and one out-breath, and count one; in, out, and count two, and so forth, until you reach ten. Once you have reached ten then count backwards to one. Keep in mind that the point is not getting to ten but staying connected to your breath.

If you experience physical discomfort sit with that for a while. If it persists then just mindfully shift your sitting posture slightly until the pain is relieved. Your "sitting muscles" (mental and spiritual as well as physical) will get stronger after some practice. Even if you sit for just five minutes, do so each morning and each evening, without question. It doesn't have to be perfect, but it is important that you do it. And I guarantee your life will change, and you will begin to experience healing and transformation.

Walking Meditation

Periods of sitting meditation can be interspersed with walking meditation. Walking meditation is similar to sitting, with the difference that we are now bringing our footsteps and our breath together; we coordinate our steps with our breathing. With each in-breath we take a step, and with each out-breath we take a step. In, out, in, out. We walk slowly and deliberately, not forcing a relationship between steps and breath, but allowing a harmonious relationship to develop.

If we are in a group, we walk in a line, one behind the other. You can let your hands hang down at your sides, or you can try the following more traditional hand position. Make a fist with your left hand with the thumb inside. Hold this fist with the palm facing in the direction of the solar plexus, the thumb joint facing upward. Then place your right hand over and around your left fist, so that the left knuckles rest inside the right palm. Maintain this position as you walk, keeping your forearms parallel to the floor. You can also place your hands in gassho, that is, palms pressed together just in front of your face with the tips of the second finger at a height even with the tip of your nose. Let your gaze rest several feet in front of you.

Walk just to walk. There is no place to arrive. You are always here and now. Be aware of how your feet meet the floor. We communicate through our feet with the earth and the entire universe. Especially in times of upset and worry, walking meditation is a wonderful tool to help us stay centered and focused and not be carried away by our thoughts, feelings, and perceptions. If you want to meditate for long periods of time, walking meditation is a wonderful way to break up your sitting time, relaxing and stretching the body. Just slow down and pay attention to your breath and your steps.

When doing walking meditation outside, follow the same guidelines, but walk a bit more quickly, connecting yourself to the pace of the larger world, of daily life. For example, breathe in for three steps and out for three steps, keeping in mind that the intention of walking meditation is always to allow for a natural rhythm of breath and steps to establish itself. (I've found that my natural rhythm is four steps with each in-breath and four steps with each out-breath.) While walking allow yourself to experience the environment that you are moving through, that you are a part of. Notice how the air caresses or cools. Notice the colors that you move through and your relationship to them, notice the sounds and your relationship to them. Walk, breathe, and notice.

Working Meditation

Work is part of our lives; it is an expression of our creativity, of our connectedness with life. There are always things to be done, so we might as well use these opportunities to practice. The shortest instruction for working meditation is: If you are not connected with your breath, you are not practicing working meditation! When we work, we work just to work. We just do what is in front of us to do. And at the end of a period of working we just step back and see what's been accomplished.

Be aware of every detail of your work. Be aware of what you perceive to be pleasant or unpleasant. Be aware of your concepts of hierarchy. Recognize when and where you feel off balance and take a step toward more balance. For example, if you are someone who always works alone, ask someone for help. If you keep yourself mostly on the side and let others take initiative, then be a little more assertive. If you have a tendency to work too quickly, slow down.

A Chinese monk said: "A day without work is a day without food." Remember that our work supports us, makes our lives possible—that without an active engagement in daily life, such simple necessities as food will not magically appear. We can think of our work as a way to say thanks to the world for providing shelter, food, light, warmth, water, and so forth. Unfortunately work has become a tremendous source of suffering in our society. Our worth, social acceptance, and belonging are often measured by what kind of job we have or whether we have a job at all. Working meditation can help us bring the light of awareness and compassion into the world of work.

Eating Meditation

We all have to eat, but often we don't pay much attention to when, what, and with whom we are eating. Eating in itself can become a drug that numbs our feelings and prevents us from waking up. The best preparation for eating meditation is to be hungry and to know that less is often more. When you sit down with a plate of food, before you begin eating, take a moment and breathe consciously three times, in and out. Then recite a verse out loud or internally:

> This food is a gift of the whole universe, the earth, the sky, and much hard work. May we live in a way that makes us worthy to receive it. May we transform our unskillful states of mind, especially our greed. May we take only foods that nourish us and prevent illness. We accept this food so that we may realize the path of practice, of love, compassion, and peace.

Then start eating. If possible, eat in silence. Chew each bite of food fifty times or at least, in the beginning of this practice, make your best effort, realizing that the bite probably won't last that long. We tend to swallow our food very quickly. For many of us, it's the same dynamic in our lives: We don't want to chew on things; we like to consume, push them in and down. So take the time to appreciate the wonderful gift of food—the smells, tastes, looks, sounds.

With children, you can start the meal by naming the foods on the table. Adults often benefit from not naming an object of food so as not to invite the intellect immediately to take over. Make the choice that helps you to fully experience the food you eat.

Rather than just eating for pleasure, consider the health of your body and mind. Food is only healthy if there is a beneficial balance; too much doesn't work, too little doesn't work. Take fifteen minutes at each meal to practice eating meditation and your body will actually have a chance to inform you when it has had enough—a point we often miss. Your body will be grateful to receive food that is properly chewed, and it will be grateful not to get too much or too little. At the end of the eating meditation breathe in and out three times and say out loud or internally, "Thank you."

Deep Listening and Mindful Speech

So much of our suffering gets acted out through the ways we communicate. The practice of deep listening and mindful speech helps us to become more aware, to receive our own stories and those of others, and to bring more peace into our lives. We have to tell our stories, again and again, and listen deeply to others' so that we can stop the cycles of suffering. In chapter 6 I described a group mindfulness practice for listening and speaking. See pages 145–46 to review it. This practice is not always comfortable and easy, but it is essential to waking up.

Further Reading

Buddhism

Aitken, Robert. *Mind of Clover*. New York: North Point Press, 1984.

Batchelor, Stephen. *Buddhism without Beliefs*. New York: Riverhead Books, 1998.

Easwaran, Eknath. *The Dhammapada*. Tomales, Calif.: Nilgiri, 1986.

Fields, Rick. *How the Swans Came to the Lake: A Narrative History of Buddhism in America*. 3d. ed. Boston: Shambhala Publications, 1992.

Glassman, Bernie. *Bearing Witness: A Zen Master's Lessons in Making Peace*. New York: Bell Tower, 1998.

Merzel, Dennis Genpo. *Beyond Sanity and Madness: The Way of Zen Master Dogen*. Boston: Tuttle, 1994.

Thich Nhat Hanh. *Being Peace*. Berkeley, Calif.: Parallax Press, 1988.

———. *The Miracle of Mindfulness*. Translated by Mobi Ho. Berkeley, Calif.: Parallax Press, 1986.

The Vietnam War

O'Brien, Tim. *The Things They Carried: A Work of Fiction*. New York: Broadway Books, 1999.

Shay, Jonathan. *Achilles in Vietnam: Combat Trauma and the Undoing of Character*. New York: Scribner, 1995.

Sheehan, Neil. *A Bright Shining Lie: John Paul Vann and America in Vietnam*. New York: Vintage Books, 1989.

On Combat, War, and Violence

Barker, Pat. *The Eye in the Door*. New York: Plume, 1995.

———. *Regeneration*. New York: Plume, 1993.

———. *The Ghost Road*. New York: Plume, 1996.

Gilligan, James. *Violence: Reflections on a National Epidemic*. New York: Vintage Books, 1997.

Grossman, Dave. *On Killing: The Psychological Cost of Learning to Kill in War and Society*. New York: Back Bay Books, 1996.

Hedges, Chris. *War Is a Force That Gives Us Meaning*. New York: Anchor Books, 2003.

Victoria, Brian. *Zen at War*. New York: Weatherhill, 2000.

Other Readings on Spirituality and Transformation

Johnson, Charles. *Turning the Wheel: Essays on Buddhism and Writing*. New York: Scribner, 2003.

———. *Oxherding Tale*. New York: Plume, 1995.

Johnston, William, ed. *The Cloud of Unknowing*. New York: Image Books, 1996.

Pagels, Elaine. *The Gnostic Gospels*. New York: Vintage Books, 1989.

Acknowledgments

The writing of this book began years ago in my efforts to make sense out of a life that seemed in shambles. After some years of recovering from the despair of addictions and cleaning up much of the difficult parts of my life that were being covered over by many forms of anesthetics, I was left with the looming legacy of my role as a combat soldier in Vietnam.

At the point at which I could no longer hold the images, the sounds, the smells, the memories, the unaddressed feelings that had been hidden away, I needed to do something to help me keep a grip on my sanity, and so I wrote. I would like to express my thanks and my deep gratitude to those without whose support this book would not exist and I might not be alive.

I would like to extend my deepest thanks to Doug Abrams, my literary agent, for his skill in presenting the idea of this book to the publishing world, for his editing and his relentless pursuit of making this the best text that it could be and getting it to publication.

To Eden Steinberg, my editor at Shambhala, for her support and commitment to this project and her skill, tenderness, and meticulous dedication in helping me put together the best book possible.

To Robert Zeigler, a psychiatrist who literally kept me alive and helped me to climb out of the frozen hell of combat.

To Nancy Miriam Hawley, a social worker whose unbridled support for years helped me learn how to live in some kind of useful relationship with society.

To Thich Nhat Hanh, who gave me my voice and the foundation of the Three Treasures.

To Bernie Baisen Tetsugen Glassman Roshi, who gave me a platform from which my voice could be heard and become manifest into action.

To Wiebke KenShin Andersen, who supports me tirelessly in her capacity as my assistant and constant companion for the past five years.

There are many, many more people who deserve to be mentioned here, but that could be a book unto itself. What I can communicate is that there is no healing without community.

The Zaltho Foundation

In 1993 Claude Anshin Thomas established the Zaltho Foundation, Inc., a 501 (c) (3) nonprofit, committed to ending violence by supporting socially engaged projects in schools, communities, organizations, and families, with an emphasis on the most important ingredient, the individual. The Zaltho Foundation organizes a variety of programs, including pilgrimages, public talks, interfaith dialogues, residential retreats, and street retreats, and works with combat veterans and victims of war. In addition, the foundation supports marginalized populations such as those in prison, the homeless, the addicted, women forced into prostitution, refugees, and others.

The Zaltho Foundation also runs the Magnolia Zen Center in Mary Esther, Florida, a residential and retreat center that is dedicated to the Buddhist teaching of interconnectedness and serves individuals involved in social action by providing spiritual support and training. In addition, the Zaltho Foundation runs the Clock Tower Practice Center in Maynard, Massachusetts, a practice center dedicated to supporting individuals and families with a commitment to learning and developing the practice of mindfulness meditation in all of its many forms.

For more information, please contact:

The Zaltho Foundation, Inc.
PMB Box 312
60 Thoreau Street
Concord, MA 01742
Phone: (978) 369-4342
Fax: (978) 263-9051
E-mail: anshin@sprynet.com
Web site: www.zaltho.org

Magnolia Zen Center
9 Magnolia Drive
Mary Esther, FL 32569
Phone: (850) 243-8169
E-mail: anshin@sprynet.com
Web site: www.zaltho.org

Clock Tower Practice Center
c/o Andrew JiYu Weiss or Wiebke KenShin Andersen
20 Elm Street
Maynard, MA 01754
Phone: (978) 897-1187 or (978) 376-4593
E-mail: jiyu@galaxy.net *or* anshin@sprynet.com
Web site: members.aol.com/ctsangha *or* www.zaltho.org